Southern Literary Studies
Fred Hobson, Editor

LITERARY
NEW ORLEANS
in the MODERN WORLD

The courtyard of the old Brulatour Mansion at 520 Royal Street,
site of the Arts and Crafts Club in the 1920s; drawing by George
Frederick Castleden, 1929
The Historic New Orleans Collection, accession no. 1974.69.5

LITERARY
NEW ORLEANS
in the MODERN WORLD

Edited by

Richard S. Kennedy

LOUISIANA STATE UNIVERSITY PRESS
Baton Rouge

Designer: Michele Myatt Quinn
Typeface: Sabon
Typesetter: Wilsted & Taylor Publishing Services
Printer and binder: Thomson-Shore, Inc.

Grateful acknowledgment is made to Special Collections, Tulane University Libraries, for permission to use excerpts from the letters of John Kennedy Toole collected in the John Kennedy Toole Papers, Manuscripts Department, Howard-Tilton Memorial Library.

Library of Congress Cataloging-in-Publication Data

Literary New Orleans in the modern world / edited by Richard S.
  Kennedy.
      p.   cm. — (Southern literary studies)
    Includes bibliographical references.
    ISBN 0-8071-2208-4 (cloth : alk. paper)
    1. American literature—Louisiana—New Orleans—History and
  criticism.   2. Authors, American—Louisiana—New Orleans—Biography.
  3. New Orleans (La.)—Intellectual life.   4. New Orleans (La.)—In
  literature.   I. Kennedy, Richard S.   II. Series.
  PS267.N49L583   1998
  810.9′976335—dc21   97-50294
                                                                      CIP

The paper in this book meets the guidelines for permanence and durability of the Committee on Production Guidelines for Book Longevity of the Council on Library Resources. ∞

For
Peggy Prenshaw and John Idol
    Society for the Study of Southern Literature

Contents

Illustrations

Preface

In the earlier part of this century when my wife's father, Charles Henry Dickinson, lived in the *américain* section of New Orleans, the city seemed to him an idyllic spot. It had outlived the disruptions and deprivations of the Reconstruction period. Racial harmony appeared to be widespread, and a modest prosperity had returned to raise the level of comfort and enjoyment for the populace. A system of streetcars with trolleys had replaced the mule cars, the New Orleans Grand Opera Company flourished at the French Opera House, and oysters were twenty-five cents a bushel. Aunts on the Buckingham side of the family remembered the vendors, with their rhythmically intoned street cries, hawking their products—everything from strawberries to clothespoles. The Creoles, after emerging from a genteel poverty, had integrated with the American families who had moved in from the upriver farms or plantations (Devall married Dickinson, Baillio married Buckingham). Among the fashionable citizens, everyone knew French, whether descended from a Creole family or not. Courtesy and gallantry prevailed in the social scene. Young ladies went to church on Sundays, read the Bible and Josephus and the stories of Thomas Nelson Page, but were much more interested in carriage rides, ball gowns, and call-out cards. Young men of good family knew their Latin, read Walter Scott, and quoted Byron and Kipling, but preferred to give their attention to horses and debutantes. There was an aura about the city as if time had come to a pleasant pause and left it a little out of date.

The new movement in the arts and literature that had begun in Europe near the turn of the century had finally reached the United States shortly before the outbreak of World War I, but literary New Orleans seemed not to take much notice. Even the rise of realism and naturalism that had developed in the late nineteenth century had not yet made its impact as the third decade of the twentieth century began. This situation is what Julius Friend was aware of when he expressed, in the April, 1921, issue of the *Double Dealer,* a desire to drive "a pile into the mud of artistic stagnation which has been our portion since the Civil War." Although this atmosphere of time-frozen insularity was irksome to Friend, it held a strong appeal for Sherwood Anderson, who had come south in 1922, away from the pressures of Chicago to discover in New Orleans a relaxed and unhurried spirit.

This very aura is what one perceives and welcomes in certain European centers—in the hill towns of Italy like Siena, the French towns of Provence like Arles, or the cities of central Spain like Toledo. Here one finds the midday languor, the appreciation of the good things of life: food and drink are taken seriously, ease is valued, hustle is absent, the warm Mediterranean climate is absorbed, though the heat of the day is avoided in shade and siesta. This likeness is not surprising, for in New Orleans the European heritage of settlement and migration has been predominantly the mix of French, Spanish, and later Italian, to which was added the dark-skinned people of other warm climes, Caribbean and African and, as time went on, other ethnic elements that soon adapted to the locale. One can expect here inhabitants who savor the possibilities of relaxation and pleasure and have created an ethos of warmth and tolerance.

Still, New Orleans, like other American cities, underwent change as the twentieth century moved on, and its writers were urged by the *Double Dealer* and other forces toward the Modern movement in literature. But Modernism in its fullest sense—that is, in literary work that employed distorted language or the breakup and restructuring of form—never really caught on among the New Orleans writers. Free verse and a new boldness in subject matter were about as far as they went. (Tennessee Williams is the outstanding exception.) What took place was rather a turning away from the dreaminess of its peculiar romanticism and, finally, a catching up with the full flow of realism that had been the mainstream of American writing for over thirty years. Thus the direction of twentieth-century literary expression has been in the realistic portrayal of its life in novels, plays, and verse. And that portrayal was reflective of the special qualities of New Orleans culture—Mediterranean, Latin, semi-American, and ever ready to take the turn back to the dark romanticism of George Washington Cable's *Old Creole Days*. By the end of the century one finds the recurrence and transformation of this romantic strain in the Gothic fiction of Anne Rice and Valerie Martin and in the mystery novels of Julie Smith, James Lee Burke, and Chris Wiltz.

New Orleans literary expression remains, then, unique and distinctive in the same way that the city itself has retained its exotic flavor in spite of the homogenizing efforts of the tourist bureau and encroachment of the T-shirt shops that seem nowadays to creep into every spot on the globe where the curious wanderer might seek an authentic past that can never be recaptured.

This book is a sequel to *Literary New Orleans: Essays and Meditations*, published by Louisiana State University Press in 1992, which placed its emphasis on earlier New Orleans writers and then concluded with chapters on Walker Percy, William Faulkner, and Tennessee Williams, whose spirits still hover over *Literary New Orleans in the Modern World*. Expanding upon that first volume, the present work has its own emphasis in presenting the development of literary activity in the city during the twentieth century and the influence of New Orleans culture on its writers, whether they be natives or temporary visitors attracted to the unusual character of the city.

Literary New Orleans in the Modern World differs in two distinct ways from the earlier book. First, it presents a great deal of local literary history along with its accounts of selected New Orleans writers. Thomas Bonner places the *Double Dealer* in a context of New Orleans literary periodicals going back as far as *De Bow's Commercial and Financial Review* and continuing on to the current publication of the *Double Dealer Redux*. Violet Bryan's essay gives a full but compact account of African American writers in New Orleans, noticing especially the black collaborative activity in such ventures as the Black Unit of the WPA in the 1930s, the Free Southern Theater of the 1960s, BLKARTSOUTH, and the Congo Square Writers' Workshop of the 1970s. At the end of the volume, W. Kenneth Holditch selects seven contemporary New Orleans writers who represent the surge of literary activity in the final decades of this century, five of whom draw upon the New Orleans mystique, a combination of Old World charm and present-day menace, and turn it into mystery and detective novels, or Gothic fiction.

The second way the book differs strongly from its predecessor is that it stresses the African American presence as an essential element in the culture of the city, not only in Violet Bryan's piece on African American writing and David Estes' essay on the hoodoo tradition but also in the way in which blacks are seen in the literary works under discussion. Blacks are important as characters in novels by both black and white authors, but beyond that, they figure thematically in the works of the white writers. This continuing awareness exhibited by the white writers permeates this book.

When Sherwood Anderson saw stevedores at work, laughing and "playing with life," he was inspired to write his novel *Dark Laughter,* in which the Negroes became the symbol of what American whites lack in their lives—that is, the blacks were seen to be living wholly integrated lives free of the debilitating repressions that burdened the whites and free of the go-getting hustle that drained the whites of joy. Lillian Hellman, remembering her childhood nurse, Sophronia, realized that Sophronia had provided her a moral upbringing and had been a source of the strength that underlies the social criticism of her plays. Shirley Ann Grau has made the racial complexities of the New Orleans scene vividly central in her work.

Together, these two volumes, *Literary New Orleans* and *Literary New Orleans in the Modern World,* provide a literary history of the city that is both extensive and informal, written in the spirit of New Orleans itself as the city has cast its spell on these scholars and literary historians, in much the same way that it has inspired the creativity of the writers who have helped to shape its image in the American imagination.

RICHARD S. KENNEDY
Temple University

LITERARY
NEW ORLEANS
in the MODERN WORLD

Sherwood Anderson in 1924, a drawing by Hyde
Man based on a photograph by Alfred Stieglitz
Courtesy Liveright Publishing Corporation

The Most Civilized Spot in America:
Sherwood Anderson in New Orleans

WALTER B. RIDEOUT

The North, Sherwood Anderson told himself on his first night
in Mobile, Alabama, in early February, 1920, is like a hard fist; the South
is like an open, relaxed hand. To recover from a bad case of the flu the author of *Winesburg, Ohio* had fled south from wintry Chicago and the demands of the advertising copywriting job he hated; and the nearly four
months he stayed, partly in Mobile, but mostly in a beach cottage at Fair-

This essay is drawn from a forthcoming Anderson biography to be published by Oxford University Press. It was first published in somewhat different form in the *Southern
Review* (Winter, 1988). Citations from the letters of Sherwood Anderson are reprinted by
permission of Harold Ober Associates Incorporated as agents for the Sherwood Anderson
Literary Estate Trust.

hope across Mobile Bay, were "golden days." He completed his best novel, *Poor White* (1920); literally shocked by the glowing colors of a southern spring, he experimented for the first time with painting; he took trips on riverboats up the Alabama and the Tombigbee and wandered for days about the lush countryside. Late in May he spent a few days in New Orleans, where he was delighted by his first acquaintance with the French Quarter, the Vieux Carré. Then he had to return to a "hot, crowded and dirty Chicago" and the tensions of his advertising job, resolved to go back to the South and to New Orleans as soon as he could.[1]

That opportunity came in January, 1922. The previous year he had taken his first trip to France, where his admiration for French life nevertheless reinforced his conviction that he must remain an American writer, and he had published his much-praised collection of tales, *The Triumph of the Egg*. Meanwhile, his second marriage, to Tennessee Mitchell, was deteriorating, and he was by then certain that he must leave a wife he felt had entrapped him by her possessiveness. As so often with him, physical escape was a way to deal with an emotional problem and with a desire to free himself from his job for writing. Money was the key to such an escape, and that came on December 21, 1921, when he was honored in New York as the first recipient of the annual *Dial* award, just established "to acknowledge the service to letters" by some outstanding writer. The two-thousand-dollar award was designed to provide both recognition of achievement and a year's freedom for further creative work. On the evening of January 12, Anderson arrived in New Orleans for the second time.

The next day he found the perfect room to settle into in the French Quarter, to which he was now drawn because it reminded him somewhat of a twelfth-century French town he had loved. The room was on the third floor of the LaBranche Building, then a rather dilapidated complex of rooming houses, at the corner of Royal and St. Peter Streets—his entry was at 708 Royal—the building then as now a landmark because of its two rows of lacelike cast-iron balconies wrapped around the two street sides and attractive to Anderson for their delicacy and flamboyance of oakleaf-acorn design. His room was large and rather bare, but it had a big table on which to work and a fireplace with, as he wrote an artist

---

1. Sherwood Anderson to Marietta D. Finley, *ca*. June 18, 1920, in Sherwood Anderson Collection, Newberry Library, Chicago. All letters henceforth cited are in this collection.

The LaBranche Building at Royal and St. Peter Streets, where Anderson took a room on the third floor in 1922
Courtesy Grant L. Robertson

friend, Jerry Blum, "a picture of the Virgin over the mantle [*sic*] and beside it two glass candle sticks, in the form of crosses with Christs on the Cross in bronze on them," a piece of "good catholic" decor that would soon find its way into his writing. The windows ran from floor to high ceiling, and by stepping through them out onto the balcony, he could, as he often did, walk back and forth delighting in the life of the street below. He arranged with the landlady, a strong, handsome young "French Creole," that she or her husband would bring him coffee and toast in the mornings so that he could at once begin his favorite routine of writing until noon and "loafing" in the afternoons and evenings.[2]

That particular afternoon of January 13, or the following one, he sought out the office, on the third floor of a commercial building at 204 Baronne Street, of the *Double Dealer,* the little magazine started the previous January by several well-to-do young men who wanted to bring the

2. Anderson to Jerome Blum, February 2, January 13, 1922; to Marguerite Gay, January 19, 1922.

new spirit in literature to what H. L. Mencken had contemptuously called the "Sahara of the Bozart." Julius Friend, one of the editors, would recall that when Anderson dropped in from the street to introduce himself, he "was wearing a wool coat with leather buttons, a loud tie gathered in below the knot by a paste ring. He had on a velour hat and carried a blackthorn walking stick." As flamboyant as the ironwork of the balconies outside his room, he looked to Friend like "a burlesque show idea of a race horse character," but almost immediately the editors forgot his flashy clothes because of Anderson's warmth and vitality and their excitement at having a distinguished literary figure call on them so casually, telling them that he had seen copies of their magazine, liked what "you fellers" were doing, and wanted to contribute things and do anything else to help. The magazine, they felt, was "made." Over the next few weeks, off and on, Anderson would see much of the *Double Dealer* group, especially of Friend, a tall, gentle, soft-spoken man, or the short, lively Albert Goldstein, who after a spell as associate editor of the *Double Dealer* would become a reporter on the *Times-Picayune,* and of John McClure, who had come from Oklahoma and with his wife had started a bookstore in the Quarter. Years later, Friend would recall that Anderson never posed as "a great writer": "He met everyone on a personal level never the official. No one felt that he was young or old, famous or unknown, while in contact with him. The extremely vivid relationship which S. A. assumed with nearly everyone was an experience having value in and for itself. One felt himself living more vividly. The best way I can express it is to say that he had a talent for living in the present and dispensing with all the usual props used to sustain amour-propre. Consequently everyone was enthusiastic about him and concluded that Sherwood was especially interested in him or her. This was true during the contact." Then, in his memoir, Friend would add from the hindsight of years of acquaintance, "But Sherwood, I believe, cared for only a few people and none to the exclusion of his interest in his work—wives and children not excepted."[3]

This first meeting with the *Double Dealer* group showed Anderson that, as he soon wrote Mencken, this "crew [was] as pleasant a crowd of

3. Julius Friend, "The Double Dealer: Career of a 'Little' Magazine," quoted in Leland H. Cox, Jr., "Julius Weis Friend's History of the *Double Dealer," Mississippi Quarterly,* XXXI (Fall, 1978), 598; Friend, unpublished article on Sherwood Anderson in his possession.

young blades as ever drunk bad whiskey."[4] The editors eagerly presented Anderson with a copy of their July, 1921, issue, which contained Hart Crane's appreciative article on his work from *Winesburg, Ohio* onward, an article that he had not seen and that praised him for his honesty, lyricism, sense of nature, and "a humanity and simplicity that is quite baffling in depth and suggestiveness." Very likely, it was this same afternoon that Anderson agreed to let the editors have the first of three "Testaments," prose poems he was experimenting with, which would be printed in the next few issues of the *Double Dealer*, and he may also have promised an article on the city and the magazine.

As for New Orleans, he almost at once fell in love with it, particularly with the French Quarter. After a morning's work at the big table and lunch, often with Julius Friend, he would roam the old streets of the Quarter, then a largely working-class, French-Italian area, rundown and colorful, where cheap rents had produced a small bohemia of local artists and writers and where tourists had only begun to come. Just a block or two away from his room was green Jackson Square, faced on one side by the Spanish-style Cabildo and the plain-fronted St. Louis Cathedral, on two other sides by the long, graceful façades of the Pontalba Apartments, and open to the east toward the markets, warehouses, and wharves along the busy Mississippi. Evenings he could spend over a dinner in talk with the *Double Dealer* editors at some restaurant where, with the Italian food, red wine was obtainable in casual defiance of Prohibition, or he could wander along the wharves or walk in the ramshackle Negro section, as he had done in Alabama, loafing, watching, listening to the voices and the laughter of the blacks. Concerning them he wrote to Jerry Blum: "The one thing they constantly do for me is to rest something inside me. I've really been going like hell and sometimes at night cant chuck it and sleep. Well[,] I go where the niggers are at work and watch their bodies and my own body gets rested. There aren't any other people in America know anything about physical work. They have the key to it, the secret to it. Dont know whether or not I'm romancing, but I've a notion they know I have a somewhat different attitude toward them than most of the whites. There is a kind of something in their eyes, both men and women, something like surprise and pleasure."[5]

---

4. Anderson to H. L. Mencken, January 25, 1922.
5. Anderson to Blum, February 2, 1922.

Lyle Saxon, journalist and popular historian, who became known as "Mr. New Orleans"
The Historic New Orleans Collection, accession no. 1988.153.27.23.4

Whatever the degree of romantic self-deception Anderson half-recognized in himself, he was as genuinely drawn to blacks as he was to the raffish characters of the Quarter, to the French and Italian workers, and to any other persons and groups outside conventional middle-class society, like the bums and flashy people who hung around the New Orleans horse racetrack, where he sometimes went more to talk than to watch the races. New Orleans, this half-foreign city at the southern "lip of the continent," at once excited and soothed him with its color, its culture, its slowness of tempo, and its warmth, in contrast to cold and frenetic Chicago, with the eagerness of so many of its people to be individuals.[6] The homogeneous French had impressed him as being, at the same time, individuals. On one of his most memorable days—it was January 28, and sunshine brought the temperature up to about 60 degrees—he wrote all morning, after lunch watched Mike Algero of the French Market win the world championship for oyster shucking before a crowd of thirty thousand in Lafayette Square, in the late afternoon walked along the docks on the riverfront "among singing negro laborers," and with Albert Goldstein that evening, "under the stars in an open air arena," saw Panama Joe Gans, the Negro middleweight champion of the world, knock out Oscar Battiste, the Negro middleweight champion of the Midwest, in the second of fifteen scheduled rounds. It was a day to write about, and he did so both in a joyous letter to his brother Karl and in his article "New Orleans, The *Double Dealer* and the Modern Movement in America," for the March issue of the magazine.

On the way down to New Orleans he had already decided to put an almost completed novel, "Ohio Pagans," aside as unsatisfactory, and instead he went immediately to a new and unusual work he had begun in one form late in his Fairhope stay and had been actively thinking about again at least since the Paris visit, when escape from business had been so often on his mind. From the beginning, he was certain that the book should be part realistic, part fantasy in mode and that it should be written in "a quick nervous prose that will have in it something of the intense nervousness of modern life while it, at the same time, strikes at what seem to me the diseases of modern life."[7] Soon he had the title he wanted: *Many Marriages*.

Day after day, the words rushed out of him. Usually, he kept to his regular schedule of writing only in the morning, but sometimes he was so seized that he wrote all day until he was "almost too weak to walk." By mid-February he had written fifty thousand words and could explain to a friend that the book was "an effort to go deeper into people and show their processes of thought and the effect of their thoughts, unexpressed[,] on their lives—a very interesting, delicate and difficult thing to do."[8]

6. Anderson to Gay, January 19, 1922.
7. *Ibid.*
8. Anderson to Marietta D. Finley, February 15, 1922.

Many Marriages, which is about a man's liberation, was itself an act of liberation for its author. The concerns of the book were much on Anderson's mind even when he was not at his writing table, and "real life" tended to flow into and feed his imaginative life, as when looking at the picture of the Virgin and the candlesticks in the room before his eyes became part of his hero's nightly ritual. Julius Friend would recall that during Anderson's two-month stay in New Orleans he "talked a good deal about Freud," though Friend was "sure he never read the books and that he got Freud second hand."[9] Judging by Anderson's description of the "great well of silent thinking" in each person, it would appear that his view of the Freudian unconscious and the means by which its contents may enter consciousness was, if secondhand, also modified to fit his notion of the imagination and its health-giving capacities; but his active concern with Freud suggests again how much *Many Marriages* was an exploration of his own psychic depths as well as those of American society, as he saw it. Further, Anderson had met and often walked and talked with Jane Webster, one of his main characters in the novel or, rather, with the young woman who was clearly her real-life prototype.

This person was Adaline Katz, the small, dark-eyed daughter of a New Orleans banker and a very southern lady "who wanted a butterfly [as a daughter] and got a grub."[10] She had graduated from Sophie Newcomb College, had taken an M.A. at Columbia University in 1920, and in fall, 1922, would go north to study for a Ph.D. in English literature at the University of Chicago. She was living in her parents' home but rebelliously would "sneak away" to the Quarter whenever she could, dropping in often at the *Double Dealer* office, probably the place where she first met Anderson. Years later, she would recall herself as being then a very dull, withdrawn, walled-up person whom Anderson perceived as one of the "waifs and strays" who needed to be brought out from behind the wall; so he concentrated on her out of everyone else in the Quarter and, by their relationship, helped greatly to bring her to emotional self-awareness. Naïve, repressed, but as obscurely eager for life as a girl in an Anderson story, she was at once deeply drawn to this man old enough to be her father, a famous writer, a physically attractive man with heavy shoulders, a ruddy complexion, tousled hair, and "wonderfully soft" brown eyes, an

9. Friend, article on Sherwood Anderson, 4.

10. The quotations and the information in these two paragraphs on Adaline Katz Samuel are from conversations with the author, December 12–13, 1959.

exotic even in the Quarter, with his battered brown tweed suits and blackthorn walking stick. She felt he was a "conductor of warmth," like his stories, someone who gave warmly to others, making "them the sponges rather than being one himself." By mutual consent there was no sexual affair, though with characteristic honesty she would later admit that such would have been fine and rewarding, very good for her. But even though no sex was involved, this Platonic relationship had otherwise all the emotional quality of a sexual affair. Thoroughly masculine in his psychology, he was, she would later term him, "an emotional stallion, not a physical one."

Anderson and Adaline sometimes lunched or dined together at Guy's, a little French restaurant with a cheap table d'hôte, on Royal Street near his rooming house; and when she took an attic room in the Pontalba Apartments for five dollars a month, a room that had been inhabited by an Italian family who had kept chickens and a goat there, he cheerfully lugged up bucket after bucket of water and helped her scrub the floor clear of droppings and clean the windows. In return, Adaline copyedited the manuscript pages of *Many Marriages*, correcting Anderson's uncertain spelling and punctuation but never changing his writing in any other way, since she knew that he loved both words in general and the words he had written. But most of all, the two had an "ambulatory relationship." Both loved the river and walking on the levees day or night, the levees like the Quarter itself then being safe even for a woman to walk around alone at any time. They knew and enjoyed talking with the bums who sat on the benches in Jackson Square or lived in shacks by the levees, and they happily watched the black stevedores singing and laughing in contests at unloading ships.

He gave her a copy of *Mid-American Chants*, in which he had written new poems, and his own copy of *Winesburg, Ohio*, which he had filled with notes, and during the year after he left New Orleans he wrote her enough letters to fill "a large carton" together with "some unpublished poems and the unfinished manuscript of a novel."[11] She would treasure these and the memory of one of the most alive and aware men she would ever know.

Over the many years to come, Julius Friend "never saw Sherwood so

---

11. Unfortunately, all this material was lost when Dr. and Mrs. Samuel's house at Bay St. Louis, Mississippi, was blown away by a hurricane in the summer of 1948.

radiant and vital as he was that winter in New Orleans." As always when his writing was going well, Anderson could feel the words flowing steadily from his mind down through arm and hand onto sheet after sheet of paper, a sensation that gave him physical and emotional well-being. He had friends to play with, black and white dockworkers to watch, the whole warm lazy life of the Quarter to step into at will. The Quarter had not been overwhelmed by industrialism as had the cities of the North; it was "surely the most civilized spot in America," he wrote his brother Karl, urging him to come for a visit.[12]

Word of his literary fame kept coming in from the outside world to heighten his satisfaction; he "already had more recognition than [he had] expected in a life time." He had read Paul Rosenfeld's "beautiful" article on his work in the January *Dial* before going to New York, but the thought of it still filled him with gratitude for its understanding and love. The last few reviews of *The Triumph of the Egg* were appearing, all strongly favorable. The book was even selling, his publisher Ben Huebsch wrote him, not tremendously but "spreading out—orders are coming from all quarters." A second printing had been required in December and then a third in February. The Modern Library edition of *Winesburg* was going into a second printing in March, and Sherwood told Karl that this edition had sold in a month as many copies as the Huebsch one had in its first year. Anderson's "I'm a Fool," in the February *Dial*, had begun to attract the interest that would eventually make it one of his most popular tales. The time in New Orleans was, in sum, a condition of happiness. Anderson felt of himself that "surely few men have been so blessed of the gods."[13]

The happiness spilled over into his essay "New Orleans, the *Double Dealer,* and the Modern Movement in America."[14] Written in late February and early March, it was a hail and farewell to the city he had come to love. Within his own lifetime, he writes, the United States has accepted a "standardization of life and thought" unknown in his father's day or even now, among the individualistic French. Against this standardiza-

12. Friend, article on Sherwood Anderson, 1; Anderson to Karl Anderson, February 1, 1922.

13. Anderson to B. W. Huebsch, February 6, 1922; Huebsch to Anderson, February 23, 1922; Anderson to Karl Anderson, February 1, 1922.

14. Sherwood Anderson, "New Orleans, the *Double Dealer,* and the Modern Movement in America," *Double Dealer,* III (March, 1922), 119–26.

tion, mirrored in the technically skilled but empty stories of the mass magazines, is set the Modern Movement, which "is really no more than an effort to re-open the channels of individual expression." Are our American lives, dedicated as they are to the merely quantitative goals of "progress," worth living? Only if America begins "to turn more of its natural vitality into the Arts, and if we begin to think more of quality than of quantity and more of living than of accumulating." Here in the "Vieux Carré," the "Old Quarter," this modern knowledge has, paradoxically, been a traditional one, and the *Double Dealer*, which proclaims the "Modern Spirit," merely reasserts the real meaning of culture; "first of all the enjoyment of life, leisure and a sense of leisure . . . time for a play of the imagination over the facts of life . . . time and vitality to be serious about really serious things and a background of joy in life in which to refresh the tired spirits."

Anderson's conclusion that "the Modern Spirit" means "putting the joy of living above the much less subtle and . . . altogether more stupid joy of growth and achievement" came to him naturally after the climactic event of his stay in New Orleans. Mardi Gras fell on February 28 that year, and though the weather was gray, the streets were filled with maskers who, Prohibition being little observed, were "properly gay and at least half abandoned to fun." Leaving his desk early, Anderson wrote a friend, he

> went . . . to play with the crowd and at noon met some friends. We went off to the old French Market to an Italian restaurant and ate, drank and danced all afternoon. The party went on no doubt half the night but at dusk I lit out to go into the negro section and walk there.
>
> It is because of the negroes, the French and the Italians that there is play to be had here.[15]

The party was over, and around March 4 Anderson had to head back to the winter-bound industrial North, leaving "openhanded" New Orleans for that "tense closed" fist, Chicago.

Four months later he permanently left Tennessee Mitchell, went off to New York, and there met Elizabeth Prall, who ran the Doubleday bookstore and had briefly employed and liked a young Mississippian named William Faulkner. Anderson, who needed a woman in his life, persuaded

15. Anderson to Finley, March 1, 1922.

Elizabeth that they should marry as soon as he was divorced from Tennessee. Divorce at that time could be most quickly obtained by brief residence in Reno, Nevada; but Tennessee's opposition was such that Anderson had to reside in Reno for more than a year, during which time he wrote that extraordinary story "The Man Who Became a Woman" and one of his best books, the fanciful autobiography *A Story Teller's Story*. On April 4, 1924, the divorce was finally declared; he and Elizabeth were married on April 5; and for the next three months they lived with her family in Berkeley, California. Then they decided to settle in New Orleans, and he went on ahead.

Back in his beloved city, Anderson moved at once into a three-room furnished apartment that had already been taken for him by Lillian Friend Marcus, sister of Julius Friend and manager of the *Double Dealer*. The apartment at 504 St. Peter Street, was a second-floor, corner one on the "uptown" (toward Canal Street) side of the block-long, red brick Pontalba Building. He had expected to be joined by Elizabeth and his older son by his first marriage, but a telegram announced that they were still in Berkeley and that she was nursing a very sick Robert. Disturbed by the boy's illness as well as by the addition of doctor's bills to his other financial problems, Anderson quickly arranged for the energetic Mrs. Marcus, who also managed the Modernist Lecture Bureau from the *Double Dealer* address, to set up speaking engagements for him. He began writing three lectures, which he entitled "Modern American Writing," "The Modern Movement in the Arts," and "America: A Storehouse of Vitality."

When Bob was well enough to travel, Elizabeth and he left Berkeley and reached New Orleans around July 15, on the same day that galley proofs for *A Story Teller's Story* arrived. Mornings, Anderson immersed himself in reading the proofs, while in the afternoons and evenings all three joyously immersed themselves in the sights, sounds, smells, and tastes of the Quarter with its narrow, noisy streets, Creole restaurants, delicate or flamboyant ironwork balconies, bright semi-tropical flowers and palm trees, the French Market, the levees and loading wharves along the Mississippi. Elizabeth was "immediately enthralled" by the city that Anderson declared "the most cultural town in America," one where people "know how to play a little."[16] The weather was moistly, drip-

16. Anderson to Mencken, *ca.* July 12, 1924.

The Upper Pontalba Building at Jackson Square, where Anderson moved into a three-room furnished apartment in 1924
Courtesy Grant L. Robertson

pingly hot in the early summer, but none of them minded the heat, and Sherwood even claimed that, like an old horse, he went better in it. By July 24 he had finished reading proofs and on that day returned them together with wording for the lengthy subtitle of the book, with its warning that fact and fancy were mixed therein, and for the dedication: "To Alfred Stieglitz, who has been more than father to so many puzzled, wistful children of the arts in this big, noisy, growing and groping America, this book is gratefully dedicated."

Three days later, on the morning of Sunday, July 27, having gone back to working on the lectures, he "suddenly shot off into a novel theme" that "pour[ed]" from him "like a flood . . . something like 28000 words in 10 days." Possibly he was prompted by remembering one of his fierce and friendly arguments in Berkeley with Elizabeth's brother, the philosopher David Prall, and wanted to assert in dramatic form convictions about the "immaturity" of America and Americans that he had long held. Certainly he was affected simply by being in New Orleans again, where *Many Marriages* had poured out of him in a similar rush. At any rate,

13

what he quickly was "going like hell on" was not exactly a novel but, as he wrote brother Karl, "a kind of fantasy of modern life—the War, sex reactions in America, artists, labor, factories. Am trying to make them all dance to slow music." It was, he wrote in other morning warm-up letters as the work progressed, "unlike anything I've done . . . all 'here and now' "—an attempt "to get and give just the slow after effect of war hatred on the emotions of people." The characters were to be not the "more or less naive simple people" he had "always written about" but people, "neither simple or naive," who were being affected by postwar "European moods" of cynicism and sophistication. The theme was so complex and "elusive" that he had "to work into a new style to fit [it]." As for the title, he quickly rejected "The Golden Circle," tentatively tried "The Lovers," and by early September had settled, temporarily, on "Love and War" or "perhaps 'War and Love.' "[17] The novel would eventually be published with the title *Dark Laughter.*

One aspect of New Orleans that Anderson especially liked and that would soon work its way into the book was the life of the blacks, at least as he perceived it:

> You walk a block to the Mississippi. Big ocean steamers [are] coming and going. The niggers are working, laughing, sweating and singing. They have the real flare for physical things. One of them rolls a heavy barrel up and down a sharp incline. He plays with it as a cat with a ball—never letting it quite get out of hand. In all handling of heavy loads in difficult places they are as clever as a good boxer. The load never quite gets the upper hand. When it is on their shoulders or heads there is a remarkable play of the body muscles, giving to the load—controlling it. Often a negro with a heavy load walking on a narrow plank does a little dance step to show he has the upper hand. . . . I have come to have a real feeling of nearness—not to any particular negro but to them all. They rest me, playing with life as they do.

His "feeling of nearness" to blacks as a kind of concrete abstraction indicates how explicitly primitivistic his attitude had become; in his book the Negro would not be a personality but a symbol of what whites lacked.

17. Anderson to Roger Sergel, early August, 1924; to Karl Anderson, early August, 1924; to Ferdinand Schevill, late September, 1924; to Otto Liveright, September 7, 1924; to Huebsch, *ca.* September 16, 1924.

"What one gets down here, at least I do," he wrote the poet John Gould Fletcher around late July, "is a kind of impersonal touch with life. What we whites seem so to have lost[,] the power of doing—the power of feeling, sensing each other[—]the blacks seem to have. Perhaps their animal suffering in the past has done it. They laugh, rub shoulders with each other, love like healthy animals, are no neurotics."[18] What whites had lost was, of course, a sense of the self as an integrated whole.

Yet another element he was writing into his book was the postwar expatriate experience, a kind of life that he decried to an interviewer from the *Times-Picayune* shortly after his arrival in New Orleans. The American expatriate is "an unhappy creature" whose vehemence of attack on "the turmoil of life in this country" betrays his regret at exile. Ironically, expatriates can find most of what they are looking for in New Orleans, "the only city in America which the factory has not spoiled [with] grime and dinginess" and with "the futile 'gogetter' spirit which spends itself in hustling around, accomplishing nothing." America "is the place for Americans to live, whether they are artists or not," but New Orleans, Anderson insisted enthusiastically to the receptive interviewer, "offer[s] the greatest field for the writer and painter of any in the United States."[19]

It was all falling together as he could wish—heat, blacks, the city, the "rich find" of love with a woman "not afraid of herself . . . the first woman who has had always something to give [him]," "the dance of the book," "often 3 or 4,000 words a day . . . until [he] could not sit at the desk any more and all [his] body trembling."[20] Huebsch might not be selling his books effectively, but he had confidence that when *A Story Teller's Story* came out in October, it should go well and his nagging money worries be eased. Meanwhile, he had just had comforting proof that other publishers were eager to take on his work, and interest in translating him into foreign languages had spread, he learned, to Japan. The Women's Club in New Orleans refused to engage the immoral author of *Many Marriages* for a lecture; but his literary fame warranted the *Times-Picayune* interview, and—a sign that at least New York was recovering from the shock of that book—the August issue of *Vanity Fair* could carry

18. Anderson to Alfred Stieglitz, September 4, 1924; to John Gould Fletcher, late July, 1924.

19. Edward R. Gay, "Well Known Author Finds Field for Artists Here," *Times-Picayune*, August 3, 1924, B-1, p. 2.

20. Anderson to Stieglitz, May 26, July 26, August 3, 1924.

Samuel Hoffenstein's "Love in Lettuce, Ohio," a lighthearted spoof of small-town sexual complexes "Recounted in the Manner of the Realistic Middle-Western Novelist," illustrated with a photograph of Anderson, the "most widely discussed of [this] school."

There was no doubt about his fame among the writers, artists, and intellectuals who gathered around the Quarter, the *Double Dealer*, the *Times-Picayune*, and Tulane University. In her autobiography, *Miss Elizabeth*, his new wife would present a sharp, if composite, memory of certain evenings with Anderson that summer and in the ensuing months:

> It was a social and congenial time, with clusters of people meeting to eat at one of the less expensive restaurants, such as Galatoire's, dining on hot, spicy foods which were complemented by cold wines. Later, everyone would move over to a place called Max in the Alley, a newspaper hangout, with a large ceiling fan that languorously revolved, stirring flies into brief action and casting moving shadows on the walls. It is a scene that is still vivid in my memory, all the men dressed in rumpled, messy seersucker suits, patched with perspiration and giving the curious effect of a group of people sitting about in white pajamas. There would be William Spratling, looking as slight and dark as a Mexican, with his jutting jaw and eyes that squinted half defiantly at the world; Fran[z] Blom, the anthropologist, with lank brown hair drifting casually over his high forehead and his light-colored eyes staring as if in interested amazement; Oliver La Farge, thin and spindly, all head and thick glasses; Roark Bradford, looking preoccupied and harassed as if all the news of all the world filtered through his active mind into the *Times-Picayune*, which he edited; Hamilton Basso, lithe and handsome with a flashing grin that was startlingly white against his dark tan; Lyle Saxon, who looked aristocratically remote even in a seersucker suit that dared not rumple when worn by him. . . . And there would be Sherwood, massive and burly as a bear, with his light cotton jacket twisted and wrinkled impossibly. Sherwood was the only one of them who had an established literary reputation in those days and the younger writers gravitated to him and usually deferred to him, even in the matter of seating, for he was the center of the conversation, always.

Although this composite memory would be written down many years after the collapse of Elizabeth and Sherwood's marriage, it is significant that her focus is on appearances (especially clothing), Lyle Saxon's elegance, much like that of Stark Young's, and Anderson's dishevelment.

She would recall also how, when New Orleans debutantes would come to visit Sherwood's favorite cafés, "he thought nothing of unbuttoning his shirt and grabbing one of them to dance with him." Already she was recognizing that her new husband, "an impulsive and generous man," was "inclined toward extravagant gestures" and that she must tactfully "temper his rashness" when she felt that he "was going too far."[21] Her own impulse toward orderly management would later come increasingly to bear on and irritate him, but mostly this summer was intensely happy for them both.

If Anderson was always the center of conversation during their social evenings, it was not simply that others deferred to his status as a writer but also that they provided a constant, enraptured audience for his stories. The constant availability of such attention was yet another reason why the summer of 1924 in New Orleans was an emotional peak in Anderson's life. Because of the intensity with which he worked on *Dark Laughter* through a steamy August, he had one of his "little bad times" at the beginning of September. But the depression was a brief one, and he was soon back creating "a new free form" for his book and even taking notes toward a series of sketches on the tone of life in the present-day South for a book to resemble Turgenev's *Annals of a Sportsman.* In mid-September, *Dark Laughter* was about half done, and he drove so hard at it in hopes of finishing by fall before his lecture engagements began that by September 23, with occasional tropical rains bringing cooler days and nights, he was two-thirds through the first draft and hoping to finish in October. On or about September 15, Sherwood and Elizabeth moved from their first apartment to one being relinquished by the impeccably dressed Lyle Saxon, a feature writer on the *Times-Picayune,* who was leaving the city in order to be in a quiet place for his own fiction writing. It was on the third and fourth floors of the Pontalba Building, 540B St. Peter Street near the corner of Chartres. There they faced onto green and flowering Jackson Square with the austere, three-spired front of St. Louis Cathedral at their left, Clark Mills's prancing equestrian statue of General Andrew Jackson in the center of the square at their right. From their windows they could look down on the square, the Quarter, the city, the curving river. It was "the loveliest view in America," Anderson insisted.

21. Elizabeth Anderson and Gerald R. Kelly, *Miss Elizabeth: A Memoir* (Boston, 1968), 83–84, 89, 82.

At last they could hang their paintings and unpack their books. Saxon let them use what Sherwood called his "magnificent" furniture rather than putting it in storage, and Anderson bought a huge old carpenter's bench, covered it with green billiard cloth, and had a desk big enough to spread out his writing projects on. After a week's flurry they were settled in even to finding, shortly, a black cook, a feisty little woman named Josephine, who kept the apartment in "shining" order when she was not preparing rich, spicy Creole dishes.

All this social living cost money, however. The rent of $110 a month for the new apartment alone was nearly double what they had been paying. Early in August, Anderson had warned Huebsch that he must soon request an advance of $1,000 against future royalties on *A Story Teller's Story*, and in mid-September he did request and receive it. There were smaller amounts coming in as well—$225 from the German publisher Insel-Verlag and $120 from the reprint of the Modern Library edition of *Winesburg*—but by the end of September, the Anderson's finances were being stretched. Lillian Marcus had at last arranged half a dozen lecture engagements, but these were mostly for late fall and early winter, and in any case Anderson could not command the top prices of a professional speaker, settling instead on a fee of $100 a lecture plus expenses or $150 if he paid his own expenses. "Lordy," he wrote Huebsch about October 4, "I wish I had this financial problem off me. It's a pest."[22]

At this point Elizabeth resolved that she must somehow help out. Among the new friends the Andersons had made were Marc Antony and Lucile Godchaux. Lucile was a lively, liberated woman whose wealthy family had repudiated her because she was living in the Quarter with Marc before marriage. Neither writers nor intellectuals, both much admired Sherwood; and Lucile had got in the habit of taking long afternoon walks with him around the Quarter or sitting on the levee with him while he talked about the characters in *Dark Laughter* as though they were living people. "Do you know," he would begin, "what kind of trick that [naming a character] did today?" Elizabeth and the Antonys decided to start an interior decorating shop. Elizabeth had her bookselling experience, and Lucile was a fairly accomplished painter, but unfortunately neither they nor the then-inexperienced Marc understood the decorating business. When they opened the Leonardi Studios at 520 St. Peter Street

22. Anderson to Huebsch, *ca.* October 4, 1924.

around early October, they ran it "along languid, leisurely lines," having fun and meeting new friends but making no money. By the end of October, Anderson had resolved that if *A Story Teller's Story* sold, he would "insist she get out."[23]

But this was in the future. By late October, 1924, Anderson had finished a first draft of *Dark Laughter,* and he quickly turned to writing some short tales that were "crowding his mind." The inspiration for the first he soon finished appeared literally at his door in the person of Elizabeth's former bookstore salesman, William Faulkner. With the financial help of his friend-mentor-manager Phil Stone, Faulkner had recently contracted with the Four Seas Company for the publication of his first book, *The Marble Faun,* writing poems having been one of the occupations interesting him far more than tending to his duties as the U.S. postmaster at the University of Mississippi. Keeping up with contemporary literature interested him more, too, and he had been particularly impressed by Anderson's tales in *Horses and Men* (1923). Except for Conrad's *Heart of Darkness,* he wrote his friend Ben Wasson, "I'm a Fool," in Anderson's volume, was "the best story he knew." Apparently, in late October he visited Wasson at the latter's home in Greenville, on the Mississippi, and while the two sat on the grassy levee one afternoon, Faulkner read the Anderson story aloud. When he finished reading, he told Wasson emphatically that he would like to meet the author, and Wasson urged him to go to New Orleans, see Elizabeth again, and through her be introduced to her husband. Fortunately, Faulkner's career as one of the less dutiful postmasters in the history of the postal service was officially ended on October 31, after an investigation of his office by an appalled inspector; much relieved at his release from a job he had detested, he left within hours for New Orleans.[24]

When Faulkner called on Elizabeth in the Anderson apartment, almost certainly on the afternoon of November 1, a Saturday, he had not expected to meet Sherwood. But Anderson was at home, the two men liked each other at once, and the Andersons invited Faulkner to stay to dinner, they having generously got into the custom of having the often impoverished writers and artists of the Quarter in for a Saturday meal.

23. *Ibid.,* 107–108; Lucile Godchaux Antony, conversation with the author, December 9, 1959; Anderson to Paul Rosenfeld, October 28, 1924.

24. Joseph Blotner, *Faulkner: A Biography* (New York, 1974), I, 367–68; Ben Wasson, *Count No 'Count: Flashbacks to Faulkner* (Jackson, Miss., 1983), 71–72.

Another guest that evening was Hamilton Basso, who at twenty was still studying law at Tulane but was bent on becoming a writer. Rather awed by the twenty-seven-year-old Faulkner, Basso listened to his talk of the northern Mississippi delta region and admired "his beautiful manners"—Faulkner was clearly on his best behavior for the Andersons— "his soft speech, his controlled intensity, and his astonishing capacity for hard drink." Basso would recall that dinner in an article memorializing Faulkner after his death, an article that also briefly memorialized his host, the "Royal Personage" among the young painters and writers of the Quarter: "We owed him much. All of us were young enough to profit by example, and Anderson's example, leaving aside the example of the artist, was basically that of benevolence. What he had, he shared. What was his to give, he gave—his time, his patience, his attention, and, rather like a canopy spread over all of these, the hospitality of his house."[25]

In his carefully detailed biography of Faulkner, Joseph Blotner has filled in a part of the contemporary social history of New Orleans that Anderson would very shortly draw on for his tale about a young man named David, who is Faulkner after Anderson's fancy had played over the real-life person. Only steps away from the Anderson apartment, in a house on Chartres Street, lived one Aunt Rose Arnold: a tall, ample, red-haired woman in her sixties who, years earlier, had been a news-service telegrapher in Chicago but who had moved to New Orleans and prospered as the owner of a gambling house where prostitutes or amorous couples could rent upstairs rooms. She was a shrewd businesswoman but motherly and generous, and Anderson had become acquainted with her since, more than Elizabeth did, he enjoyed talking with the "low-life" of the Quarter, the rumrunners, whores, cardsharpers, bums. In the story "A Meeting South," she appears as the "Middle Western born and bred" Aunt Sally, "a motherly soul" long since retired from her business ventures. The unnamed Ohio-born narrator first meets the young Mississippi poet David in the narrator's apartment, notices his limp as they go out to spend the evening together—a limp such as Faulkner could assume when he was role-playing—is impressed as they sit on the river's docks by David's "gift for drinking," and listens to David's tale of his serious injury while flying in France with a British squadron during the war.

25. Hamilton Basso, "William Faulkner, Man and Writer," *Saturday Review*, July 28, 1962, p. 11.

Because of the injury David lives so constantly "in the black house of pain" that he has difficulty sleeping. To manage his suffering, he drinks heavily of whiskey made by a black on his father's rundown plantation. The narrator takes David to Aunt Sally's house, where the three sit talking on her brick-paved, flower-scented patio. Aunt Sally likes David at once, understandingly furnishes him with whiskey, and listens happily while he talks of his north Mississippi country and of the blacks there. Relaxed by her presence, David lies down on the bricks and is able to sleep. "We used to have some good men come here in the old days too," Aunt Sally comments quietly, and the narrator goes out into the "soft smoky" New Orleans night, thinking of both midwesterner Aunt Sally and the pain-wracked young southern poet as aristocrats.

It is pleasant and fruitless to speculate how much of this tale came from Anderson's fancy, but it is certain that Faulkner's own imagination supplied the yarn about a flying injury in a wartime France where he had never served. Ironically, Anderson the "antirealist" seems to have transcribed this directly from what he thought to be "real" life, for later he would tell Ben Wasson that he was extremely upset to learn that Faulkner had lied to him about his war service. But this knowledge would come after the fact. The significant qualities of the tale are several: the controlled casualness of the oral narrative; the sensuous feel for the Quarter at night; the quiet intimation that "aristocracy" is a personal characteristic manifesting itself less often "above" than "below"—at any rate, outside—a convention-bound middle class; and, of course, the proof in fiction that Anderson and Faulkner did hit it off at first meeting. After a very few days Faulkner-David left for Oxford, but his visit had been so happy for him and the Andersons that he knew he was welcome back. As for the story, Anderson wrote it quickly, so quickly that he had a typed copy in the mail to his literary agent in New York by November 8, only a week after "David"'s first appearance at the Pontalba.

"A Meeting South" would be published to much praise in the *Dial* in April, 1925. During that spring, after Anderson had completed a two-month lecture tour, he and Faulkner, who had returned to New Orleans for a longer stay in January, established a close if brief friendship. In those spring months, Carvel Collins has found, the older writer read the sections of the younger one's first novel, "Mayday" (with the published title of *Soldier's Pay*), as he wrote them. Anderson was so impressed that he urged his new publisher, Horace Liveright, to accept it for publication on

the prophetic grounds that Faulkner was "the one writer here of promise" to become "a real writer."[26]

In July, 1925, Faulkner left New Orleans for his first visit to Europe.
Anderson and Elizabeth, escaping the city's summer heat, discovered the
tiny mountain community of Troutdale in southwestern Virginia, where
in 1926 he would build a stone house and settle more or less permanently,
returning to New Orleans only rarely for short visits. The paths of the
two men had intersected briefly and then diverged, Faulkner to be recognized eventually as the greatest American novelist of the twentieth century, Anderson to experience a slow decline in fame after the publication
of *Dark Laughter* in 1925 and, with exceptions such as the fine tales
"Death in the Woods" and "Brother Death," a decline in his work also.
Looking back, he could have seen that his two residences in New Orleans
had marked a kind of turning point in his career. In this "most cultural
town in America," his third marriage had gone well, he had had daily opportunity to "play"; he had had the thanks of young people, artists and
nonartists, for his generous encouragement of them; he had enjoyed local
and national fame as a leading modernist writer; and in excited out-
pourings he had written drafts of two of, if not his best, certainly his most
risk-taking experimental novels. "Openhanded" New Orleans had been
good to him.

26. Anderson to Horace Liveright, June 1, 1925.

Harnett T. Kane with Mr. and Mrs. Julius Friend
The Historic New Orleans Collection, accession no. 1983.215.61

The *Double Dealer* and the Little-Magazine Tradition in New Orleans

Thomas Bonner, Jr.

Images from Greek mythology form a trope throughout the writings and art found in the forty-eight issues of the *Double Dealer*. Unlike Athena, who sprang from the head of Zeus, the *Double Dealer* did not have a miraculous birth in New Orleans in 1921, but like Athena, its beginning had a particularly masculine aspect. How the *Double Dealer* in its essential character came to be and how this little magazine published from 1921 through May, 1926, affected the literary community in and about New Orleans and its periodicals in subsequent years give some credence to the bold claims of the editors and inform our own measure of the magazine.

Many factors came together in the formation of the *Double Dealer*. In part, the magazine evolved from a cultural force that moved the writers in post–Civil War New Orleans to establish a distance between the old Creole French culture and the rapidly developing American one. The domination of literary culture in the city by women after the war also underlay the establishment of the journal. From a wider perspective, the Victorian period and the emergence of Modernism contributed to the ambivalent attitudes expressed in its pages, especially in the editorials. The energy, if not rambunctiousness, of its founders and writers lay in the spirit of revolt brought about by World War I, an element complicated by the implications and societal memories of a defeated South. Vestiges of the New South movement remained in the editors' emphasis on regionalism. And, of course, the *Double Dealer* had a role in the little-magazine movement of the post–World War I period.

By summer, 1926, publication of the magazine was history. The *Double Dealer* served as an incubator of local literary culture and a conduit of Modernism for nearly five years. Most periodicals by their very nature are ephemeral; we see their bombastic entrances and silent departures. What happened in the aftermath of the *Double Dealer*'s demise, and how has its influence been felt among the writers and the publications that have made New Orleans home? The brief history of the journal provides a paradigm for what was to take place in the years following, when several of its editors and writers became involved in the establishment of other little magazines and local publishing houses. From decade to decade, and even in the 1990s, evidence of the *Double Dealer*'s influence lingers in the particular features of the literary journals that developed in New Orleans.

Within two months of its first issue, the *Double Dealer* received positive and negative notices in newspapers from Atlanta to Paris. During the period of its publication and in the decade after its demise, Sherwood Anderson, H. L. Mencken, and Edmund Wilson brought the magazine national attention. Scholarly attention came in a 1941 master's thesis from Tulane by Harry Durant de Ponte. A number of articles addressed its place in the little-magazine movement, generally placing it in the shadow of the *Fugitive*, from Nashville. The most sustained study of the *Double Dealer* is still Frances Jean Bowen's 1954 doctoral dissertation from Vanderbilt University. Recent commentary includes a chapter in Fred Hobson's *Serpent in Eden: H. L. Mencken and the South* (1974), in which he traces Mencken's influence on the magazine; a chapter in Violet Harrington Bryan's 1993 *The Myth of New Orleans in Literature: Dialogues of Race and Gender;* James G. Watson's 1984 article in *American Literature,* in which he builds on the New Orleans chapters of Joseph Blotner's 1974 biography of William Faulkner; and Leland H. Cox, Jr.'s 1978 essay in *Mississippi Quarterly* that discusses Julius Friend's account of the magazine. The late Michael Fanning of Southeastern Louisiana University devoted several years to the study of *Double Dealer* editor Basil Thompson and left a substantially complete experimental fictional-critical approach in manuscript. In the lyrics of a later day, the *Double Dealer* did not turn out to be "a sometime thing."

The story of this little magazine does not begin in 1921, however. Rather, it begins in *De Bow's Commercial and Financial Review* (1846–1880) and in the English-language newspapers of the city, like the *Times-Democrat* during the latter part of the nineteenth century, when New Orleans was trying to throw off its French colonial character and when newspapers across the country published stories and poems, as did the *Times-Democrat;* for example, it published four of Kate Chopin's stories and one of her poems during the 1890s. For a periodical devoted, according to its name—*De Bow's Commercial and Financial Review*—to noncultural subjects, this publication displayed a surprising interest in literary matters past and present, including the development of a strong critical edge. Articles ranged from analyses of writings by William Shakespeare and Anthony Trollope to comparisons of ancient and modern literature. A chauvinistic appreciation of southern literature emerges in comparisons of the writing with that of the North. Some essays suggest a concern with a perceived deterioration of modern taste. The attempt to provide an eclectic range of literature is evident in its genres and writers. It possessed the same muscular pose that the editors of the *Double Dealer* were to strike in later years. That many thought the South a provincial region is evident in the defensive and on occasion rebellious postures the editors assumed. The issues of *De Bow's* from the 1860s reveal a marked masculinity, as might be expected from a commercial and financial review of the time.

Despite the literary accomplishments of men like Lafcadio Hearn and George Washington Cable and the cultural histories by Charles Gayarré and Alcée Fortier, the leadership among writers in New Orleans had acquired a distinctively female character in the 1880s through and beyond the first decade of the twentieth century. Grace Elizabeth King not only produced thirteen volumes of fiction and prose, but she also established a salon on St. Peter Street in the French Quarter that still meets for weekly literary and cultural discussions. Mollie Moore Davis, whose book publications in poetry, fiction, and drama numbered more than twenty-five, maintained a literary salon that Kate Chopin visited occasionally.[1] Mary Ashley Townsend's prose and poetry appeared in newspapers, magazines, and books. Ruth McEnery Stuart published more than seventy of her short and longer works of fiction during her lifetime. And Eliza Jane Nicholson, known as Pearl Rivers in her literary publications, owned and managed the New Orleans *Daily Picayune,* a frequent publisher of literature.

One could argue that this period was the birth of American literature in New Orleans. That much of the vision and energy applied to literature in English had its source in female writers accordingly seems appropriate. Many female writers and artists contributed to the local journal *Art and Letters,* which attempted a balance among regional, national, and international issues. Its editor proclaimed in the proem of the first issue in 1887: "There exist a thousand reasons for believing that the South's intellectual leaders have something to say that is worthy of the world's attention." Its editor, according to Judith H. Bonner, was Mary Ashley Townsend, even though her name did not appear in that capacity in print. Then an event occurred that signified the closing of one history and the opening of another: Jefferson Davis' death on a visit to New Orleans in December, 1889. Aside from women organizing to commemorate the men *and the women* of the lost cause, this event brought together energies of expression both in oratory and literature that ultimately transcended the particular range of a Confederate revival. In 1894 the female editor and proprietor of *Men and Matters: A Monthly Magazine, of Fact, Fancy, and Fiction,* "Miss M. Evans," included this motto on the cover: "Our doubts are traitors, and make us lose the good we oft might win by fearing to attempt." The magazine, which like *Art and Letters* included criticism, literature, and art, had a significant number of female contributors. A dichotomy of tone and content on matters of gender emerged; for example, the February, 1897, issue included an article entitled "Of Interest to Women: Number of Females Engaged in Trying Occupations"

1. Dorothy Brown and Barbara Ewell, eds., *Louisiana Women Writers: New Essays and a Comprehensive Bibliography* (Baton Rouge, 1992), 226–27.

and a series of photographs of boats, their female names prominently identified, nearly all of them honoring the male owners' female muses.[2]

If Jefferson Davis' death jolted the creative atmosphere in New Orleans, World War I had an even greater effect. The forces of Modernism began to displace the aura of the New South, and the shadows of newly sculpted doughboys fell over those of Confederate riflemen. A long-dormant masculine energy emerged in New Orleans as bold skyscrapers began to eclipse the scattered church steeples that rose above the city. It was ironic, as the literary critic and rare book dealer Joseph Cohen noted in an interview, that men, in a reversal of their usual business and governmental roles, had become more and more closely involved in the social life of the city, especially the Mardi Gras organizations that frequently excluded Jewish gentlemen and their families. Furthermore, he said that the blossoming of literature at this time in the city had both the leadership and the financial support of Jewish men and women. Frances Bowen had earlier emphasized this prejudice as it affected Julius Friend and his wife, whom she observed as possessing "the best in Hebraic tradition, its common sense, its vitality and love of life, its humanitarian and broad art tradition."[3] Friend became the moving force in establishing the *Double Dealer* at 204 Baronne Street. Its first issue appeared in January, 1921.

In its editorial focus, the magazine reached into the past as well as toward what it thought the future would bring. Its founding editors, the cultural critic Julius Friend and the poet Basil Thompson, with associate editors Albert Goldstein and Paul L. Godchaux, do not sound very different from earlier editors of New Orleans literary magazines when they wrote that the "appeal once more is to that select audience for whom romance and irony lie not so many leagues apart; whose veneration for art, music, and letters, is not so solemn that it cannot be lightened by a sense of humor; whose opinions of society, economics, and politics are drawn,

2. *Art and Letters,* I (1887), 1; Judith H. Bonner, "*Art and Letters:* An Illustrated Periodical of Nineteenth-Century New Orleans," *Southern Quarterly,* XXVII (1989), 66; *Men and Matters: A Monthly Magazine of Fact, Fancy, and Fiction,* III (January, 1894), cover; (February, 1897), 45.

3. Joseph Cohen, conversation with the author, April 29, 1995; Frances Jean Bowen, "The New Orleans *Double Dealer,* 1921–May 1926" (Ph.D. dissertation, Vanderbilt University, 1954), 417–18. See also Frances Jean Bowen Durrett, "The New Orleans *Double Dealer,*" in *Reality and Myth: Essays in American Literature,* ed. William E. Walker and Robert L. Welker (Nashville, 1964), and Leland H. Cox, Jr., "Julius Weis Friend's History of the *Double Dealer,*" *Mississippi Quarterly,* XXXI (Fall, 1978), 589–604.

Headquarters of the *Double Dealer* on the third floor at 204 Baronne Street
The Historic New Orleans Collection, accession no. 1979.325.446

not from the perusal of dusty books, but rather from the vision of tolerant eyes estimating the devious ways of the world." The name of the magazine itself, from William Congreve's play *The Double Dealer,* reflects a
concern "with human nature, the raw stuff. . . . We mean to deal double,
to show the other side. . . . But we remain ourselves who can 'deceive

them both by speaking the truth.'"[4] And yet with all this youthful bravado (the editors were in their early to mid-twenties), they claimed Lafcadio Hearn as their muse, vowing to print his work often in forthcoming issues. Hearn's essay on the reality and romance of fencing as practiced in New Orleans graced this first issue and mirrored the editors' declarations.

An epigram in the first number suggests the tension between male and female that would persist in other numbers: "Man and woman were created to dwell together from time to time." It is ironic that funds for the founding of the magazine came from Lillian Friend Marcus, the sister of Julius. In the third number an editorial entitled "The Ephemeral Sex" seems to attack women as artists and describes them as "complete failures, pathetic nonentities." Some scholars have taken this editorial literally, seeing it as evidence confirming the journal's antifemale bias. Not all of the editorials were straightforward, however; there were frequent attempts at irony and humor, many of them failed ones, as in this item. Bowen and Bryan, however, catalog several examples that clearly demonstrate a bias against the New Woman. And yet the high number of women writing in the *Double Dealer*—three to four in each issue—partly undermines that position. An editorial in the fifth number (May, 1921), entitled "Wanted, A Hotspur: Or Is Our Man of Tomorrow to Be a Woman?" emphasizes the New Masculinity threatened by the New Woman.[5] Over the life of the journal, four women held editorial positions. A journal of men *with* women was the result.

The tension between the local and the national found expression in editorials and the material that the magazine published. One editorial (April, 1921) describes the journal as "a movement, a protest, a rising against the intellectual tyranny of New York, New England, and the Middle West." Another (May, 1921) argues against the "tincture of the soil" as a qualifying mark of American literature and calls for universality. The next number (June, 1921) argues against sentimentality in southern literature and calls for an examination of "the physical, mental and spiritual outlook of an emerging people [southerners]—the soulawakening of a hardy, torpid race, just becoming reaware of itself." At the same time, another *Double Dealer* editorial showed that the magazine

4. *Double Dealer,* I (January, 1921), 2–3.
5. *Ibid.,* I (January, 1921), 14, (March, 1921), 85, (May, 1921), 173.

sought to join with Modernism through emphasizing direct experience—the Emersonian rejection of "dusty books"—when it praised "the elemental" and pointed to "crudity" as vital in American literature. James G. Watson observes this practice at work when he refers to Faulkner's contribution, "New Orleans," as a reflection of the "basics in human life."[6]

Sherwood Anderson makes the clearest connection to Modernism in his essay "New Orleans, the *Double Dealer* and the Modern Movement in America" when he emphasizes individuality, imagination, and concrete culture as vital to Modernism, those elements being found in New Orleans and the *Double Dealer*. In his Whitman-like way, Anderson describes the presence of black people in New Orleans as a mark of a distinctive culture, represented to some extent in the magazine by the inclusion of black writers and subjects. As Violet Harrington Bryan points out, this material "reflected the new national interest in the Negro."[7] Indeed, one national publisher placed an advertisement in this issue looking for black writers and writings about blacks.

The *Double Dealer* revealed an acute awareness of the little-magazine movement with two editorials about a year apart analyzing the strengths and weaknesses of other journals, including the *Little Review* and the *Pagan,* both of which the editors had high regard for. It also carried on a conversation in its editorials about the state of short fiction, about which it was generally pessimistic. To give weight to its claim of being "A National Magazine from the South" (July, 1921, cover), the *Double Dealer* maintained correspondents in New York and Chicago as well as in Paris and Rome.[8] It participated in the recognition of Gerard Manley Hopkins, the revival of Herman Melville, and the introduction of Danko, a Nigerian poet, to a wider audience. There was even some attention given to then-marginalized social issues and writers. Despite the parade of writers who were and who would be national and international figures, the *Dou-*

---

6. *Ibid.,* I (April, 1921), 126, (May, 1921), 171–72, (June, 1921), 214, 114; James G. Watson, "New Orleans, the *Double Dealer,* and 'New Orleans,'" *American Literature,* LVI (May, 1984), 216.

7. *Double Dealer,* III (March, 1922), 119–26; Violet Harrington Bryan, *The Myth of New Orleans in Literature: Dialogues of Race and Gender* (Knoxville, 1993), 82.

8. *Double Dealer,* I (July, 1921), cover. See Fred Hobson, *Serpent in Eden: H. L. Mencken* (Baton Rouge, 1974), 33–56.

ble Dealer began a slow decline after the summer of 1922, perhaps the most extraordinary year in the Modern movement.[9]

The *Double Dealer* had become the most significant literary magazine in the Deep South during the 1920s. In a few short years, the magazine published some of the more important American writers of the century, among them Robert Penn Warren, Hart Crane, Thornton Wilder, Donald Davidson, Ernest Hemingway, Djuna Barnes, Allen Tate, and others. The combination of known and unknown writers and the enthusiasm for experimental writing (Babette Deutsch, Alfred Kreymborg) marked both its editorial character and Modernist temper. Despite its brief life, it outlasted other magazines, like the *Fugitive.*

Albert Goldstein noted correctly that the magazine's "lofty objective was realized to a degree." Although the *Double Dealer* did break away from an older tradition of sentiment, it failed to print texts as remarkable as the later reputations of its contributors. Even Hemingway commented to friends planning a magazine, "One of the most important things is to get the very best work that people are doing so you do not make the mistake of the Double Dealer and such Magazines made of printing 2nd rate stuff by 1st rate writers." James K. Feibleman, a philosopher and writer who had contributed to the magazine, observed in a similar vein that it "could boast of a number of distinguished contributors," but that "the others present [at an editorial meeting] were never heard of again. They did not succeed in getting into the stream of history."[10]

With the May, 1926, issue, which included poems by Amy Lowell and Hamilton Basso and an essay by Howard Mumford Jones, the *Double Dealer* ceased publication. Its influence, however, continued, with its ideas, editors (with the exception of Thompson, who had died), and writers appearing in new journals in the region. The *New Orleanian,* which began in 1930, picks up the Hotspur image in its opening editorial: There

9. See Lola L. Szladits, *1922, A Vintage Year: A Selection of Works from the Henry W. and Albert A. Berg Collection of English and American Literature* (New York, 1972).

10. Albert Goldstein, "The Creative Spirit," in *The Past as Prelude: New Orleans, 1713–1953,* ed. Hodding Carter (New Orleans, 1968); Ernest Hemingway, *Selected Letters, 1917–1961,* ed. Carlos Baker (New York, 1981), 145; James K. Feibleman, "Literary New Orleans Between World Wars," *Southern Review,* n.s., I (July, 1965), 704, 706. See also James K. Feibleman, *The Way of Man: An Autobiography* (New York, 1952), 266–98.

THE
DOUBLE DEALER

JUNE, 1922

CONTENTS

Vol. III   No. 18

Table of contents of the June, 1922, issue of the *Double Dealer*, which illustrates its international scope
Courtesy Judith H. Bonner, The Historic New Orleans Collection

is "no justification for the theory that we Orleanians have less energy than the inhabitants of other sections."[11]

The format of the *New Orleanian* as well as its tone of bravado and irony was similar to that of the *Double Dealer,* and its writers included John McClure, Albert Goldstein, and Roark Bradford, all of whom had been associated with the magazine. In 1935 Bennett Augustin edited the *Menagerie,* which, even more than the *Double Dealer,* had strong political interests. McClure contributed satirical fiction with images from Greek myth to this decidedly male enterprise. Even though the *Southern Review* in Baton Rouge was indebted to the *Fugitive,* it also felt the influence of the *Double Dealer;* Robert Penn Warren, one of its founders, had published in the earlier magazine and understood its dual perspective, for in 1935 the editors noted that the *Southern Review* would "aim at presenting and interpreting Southern problems to a national audience and at relating national issues to the Southern scene." The editors also applied the same criteria as the *Double Dealer* to the material it published: "significance and artistic excellence."[12] In 1940, *Iconograph,* led by editor Kenneth L. Beaudoin, appeared in New Orleans. Only Robert Tallant, through his friendship with Lyle Saxon, provided a particle of continuity with the *Double Dealer.* This mimeograph publication had some of its predecessor's political scope and self-consciousness, advertising itself as "New Orleans' Only Literary Quarterly."

In the 1950s, for the first time, there was a lull in the continuity of personal and editorial influence of the *Double Dealer.* The most significant local periodical from this decade to emerge, the *New Orleans Poetry Journal,* founded by Richard Ashman and poet Maxine Cassin, had its roots in a response to the difficulty of much contemporary poetry. Ashman, from Pennsylvania, and Cassin, just out of Newcomb College, had no contact with the former staff or writers of the *Double Dealer* and initially no awareness of the magazine's influence, but it reasserted a similar spirit. In an interview Cassin noted, "We did not look back. . . . We were more national than local."[13] The only indirect influence that might be discerned in later issues is their contact with the writer-photographer

11. Kenneth T. Knoblock, editorial, *New Orleanian,* September 6, 1930, p. 11.

12. Lewis P. Simpson, introduction to *"The Southern Review" and Modern Literature, 1935–1985,* ed. Lewis P. Simpson, James Olney, and Jo Gulledge (Baton Rouge, 1988), 18.

13. Maxine Cassin, telephone interview, May 20, 1995.

Clarence John Laughlin, who was associated with the *Menagerie*. After a lapse of more than two decades, Cassin developed the New Orleans Poetry Journal Press, which published local writers like Martha McFerren as well as national writers like Vassar Miller.

Alice Moser Rivera Claudel, who had been associated with *Iconograph* in 1940, began editing the *New Laurel Review* on the East Coast. By the early 1970s she had brought it to New Orleans. In making arrangements for republishing Hemingway's "A Divine Gesture," which had originally appeared in the *Double Dealer* more than fifty years earlier (in May, 1922), she observed that not only were the magazine and the work it published important, but the people associated with the magazine were influential as well; as she noted in an interview, they "spread their seeds" in periodicals in New Orleans for the next thirty years.[14] Under her direction the *New Laurel Review* showed a keen awareness of the South, especially New Orleans, and an acquaintance with national movements. That perspective, going back to the *Double Dealer,* continues in both the magazine's independence and the content under its current editor, Lee Meitzen Grue.

In 1980 the *Xavier Review* began a new series after a lapse of a decade of publication, before which it had been published as *Xavier University Studies*. The change in name and format reflected the influence of the *Double Dealer,* not from any personal contact with its editors or writers but from a scholarly awareness of what the magazine had accomplished in providing a meeting ground for local and national writers. Also, since 1926, no subsequent publication had successfully, over a sustained period, accomplished similar goals. Claudel's poem "Barrow Street and 17," an essay on Faulkner in New Orleans, and another on the German theater in New Orleans reflected the *Double Dealer* tradition in the first issue. At the time, the *New Orleans Review* had a clearly national focus with a strong, interdisciplinary perspective in the arts, film, and translations, but it did not envision itself then as a publication with strong interests in local content or writers. After a brief pause in publication, this journal re-emerged in 1994 under Ralph Adamo as one with strong local interests, most recently with special issues on Everette Maddox and New Orleans poets.

14. See Thomas Bonner, Jr., "Hemingway's 'A Divine Gesture': The *Double Dealer* Text," *New Laurel Review,* VIII (1978), 7–12; Alice Moser Claudel, interview with the author, May 3, 1977.

New Orleans, despite a few years of communal indifference in the 1950s, has shown itself to be a continually self-conscious literary place, even a center.[15] No better example can be found than in the new journal entitled the *Double Dealer Redux,* published by the Faulkner Society in New Orleans and headquartered at the site of Faulkner and William Spratling's apartment on Pirate's Alley in the French Quarter. The legacy of the *Double Dealer* has been principally the juncture of national and local writing in the literary publications of the past seventy years. The tension between male and female that existed throughout its brief duration has resolved into unusual cooperation between male and female writers and editors, and there have been at least two strong female editors. Its inclusion of African American voices set the stage for similarly conscious efforts by the *New Laurel Review, Xavier Review,* and *New Orleans Review.* The classical myths and references in the *Double Dealer,* including the figure of Janus on its front covers, reinforced its attempt to break beyond the provincial and into the wider American and international cultures, beyond the past and toward the future. The journal succeeded in becoming known beyond the city of its birth, and almost every literary magazine in New Orleans since the 1920s has felt the influence of the *Double Dealer,* its Hotspurs, and its Athenas.

15. See Lewis P. Simpson, "New Orleans as a Literary Center: Some Problems," in *Literary New Orleans,* ed. Richard S. Kennedy (Baton Rouge, 1992), 76–88, and Thomas Bonner, Jr., "Literary Center or Literary Place: The Ambiguity of New Orleans," *Journal of the American Studies Association of Texas,* XXV (1994), 1–13.

Hamilton Basso in 1954
Photo by George Cserna, by permission of Etolia Basso

Paris in My Own Backyard:
Hamilton Basso

INEZ HOLLANDER LAKE

When Jonathan Daniels toured the South in 1937, he described Louisiana as a "Caribbean republic" whose hard Anglo-Saxon tradition had been "softened by pleasant and relaxing Latin ways." One of America's most un-American cities, New Orleans' heritage is racially mixed, Latin, and Catholic rather than white, Anglo-Saxon, and Protestant. Notwithstanding the city's wet winters, floods, hurricanes, and its location amid the swamps, New Orleans has always remained the jewel of the Deep South. Before it was discovered by the tourist industry, the city lay undisturbed on the outer bayous of Louisiana. Slumbering in the aftermath of the Civil War and impoverished by the burdensome Reconstruction years, the elegant French Quarter had deteriorated into a slum of crime and prostitution, and although there was little to remind the visitor of the city's rich colonial past, the place had an unequivocal charm that the New England novelist Charles Dudley Warner captured when ambling downtown on an early Sunday morning in 1887:

> In the balconies and on the mouldering window-ledges flowers bloomed, and in the decaying courts climbing-roses mingled their perfume with the orange; the shops were open; ladies tripped along from early mass or to early market; there was a twittering in the square and in the sweet old gardens; caged birds sang and screamed the songs of South America and the tropics; the language heard on all sides was French. . . . Nothing could be more shabby than the streets, ill-paved, with undulating sidewalks, and open gutters, little canals in which the cat became the companion of the crawfish, and the vegetable in decay sought in vain a current to oblivion.

Warner seems to have been acutely aware of the split nature of the town; juxtaposing the picturesque and the dirty detail, he was enchanted by what he called this "thriftless, battered, stained and lazy old place."[1] It was here, in the heart of the Quarter, when Choctaw Indians still roamed the streets, that the novelist Joseph Hamilton Basso was born on September 5, 1904.

Although Basso characterized his family as "Mediterranean, Catholic [and] still essentially European," the family belonged to the New Orleans middle class that Joe Taylor describes as varying in degrees of wealth "but as a whole . . . literate, conservative, religious, and economically ambitious."[2] Hamilton's grandfather, Joseph Basso, had established a little shoe factory in their house on Decatur Street, located between Barracks Street and Hospital Street. Once the French Opera arrived in the 1880s, the family company specialized in making shoes for the stage.

Hamilton's childhood in the Quarter appears to have been particularly carefree and idyllic. The house on Decatur Street may have had a few things in common with the house that one of Basso's heroes, Jason Kent, grows up in and describes as "a rather wonderful old house" situated on "a rather wonderful street. From the attic window you could see the rooftops for miles . . . and most of the nations of Europe had managed

1. Jonathan Daniels, *A Southerner Discovers the South* (New York, 1938), 231; Charles Dudley Warner, "Sui Generis," in *The World from Jackson Square: A New Orleans Reader,* ed. Etolia S. Basso (New York, 1943), 307, 308.

2. Hamilton Basso, "William Faulkner," *Saturday Review,* July 28, 1962, p. 12.

to crowd into that one block."[3] The house of the Bassos opened onto an inner courtyard, from where Hamilton could observe the next-door neighbor, who was a poet. The boy's first encounter with this specimen from the literary world turned out to be a disappointing experience: the so-called poet was a man in suspenders who, with a notepad in his lap and a fat cigar in his mouth, sat about loafing for nearly an hour. Many years after this uneventful meeting with the poet, Basso noted that it had had its value, since it taught him that "poetry can't be hurried and that a poet may well be a bald-headed man in suspenders, smoking a cigar."[4]

As a child, Hamilton roamed around the French Quarter, where he knew all the shop owners; like his parents and grandparents, they lived on the second floor above their shops. Although he belonged to a literary crowd at school, Hamilton preferred to play after school with the tough kids or "wharf rats" on the New Orleans waterfront. Like Dekker Blackheath, the hero of his second novel, *Cinnamon Seed* (1934), he would dive for bananas thrown from the steamers. In an unpublished autobiographical sketch Basso further describes the sensation he felt as a boy when, lying awake, he heard the "whistles of the boats as they nosed cautiously through the fog." In the daytime he would walk along the wharves, and as the "smell of sugar and tar and coffee crept into his nostrils," he enjoyed the hustle and bustle of harbor activities. A similar impression of the waterfront is given in *Cinnamon Seed,* where Dekker lounges about the same wharves that Basso must have ambled along when he was a child:

> The sun was shining on the river and there were many ships. He walked down the wharves reading the names of the ships, but all the names were strange and he saw none of the sailors he knew. He knew many sailors and even a captain, Mr. Gundersonn, and one of the sailors, Mr. O'Callahan, had a man-o'-war foaming across his chest into a brush of stiff red hair. He watched the negroes loading lumber on the *Apprentice,* seating himself on

3. Hamilton Basso, *Days Before Lent* (New York, 1939), 38.

4. Hamilton Basso, "A New Orleans Childhood: The House on Decatur Street," *New Yorker,* October 9, 1954, p. 94. This story is remarkably similar to Orlando's first encounter with a poet who is equally "fat, shabby," and reluctant to put pen to paper. Like the young Basso, Orlando asks, "Was this a poet? Was he writing poetry?" (Virginia Woolf, *Orlando* [London, 1928], 14).

a hogshead in the midst of the clatter of hand-trucks, and shouting negro voices and negro bodies shining in the sun, and he was reminded of an old ambition to some day become a sailor and go to foreign places and see foreign things and fall in love with a beautiful foreign woman. He had no desire, however, to have a man-o'-war foaming across his chest.[5]

Basso clearly shared Dekker's fascination with foreign places: later, he would board the freighters he knew from his childhood and sail all over the world to write travelogues commissioned by such magazines as *Holiday* and *Life*.

We have virtually no information about Basso's adolescent years. All we know is that he was graduated from Warren Easton High School in 1922. That same year he entered Tulane University, where, in accordance with his father's wishes, he pursued a law degree.[6] Leafing through the Tulane yearbooks of the time, one discovers, besides bobbed hair and Charleston dresses, that even though Hamilton seems to have been a quiet student at first, occasionally appearing as a listed member of a debating or drama club, he gradually gained stature among friends and foes.

Grandly situated in an uptown neighborhood, the Tulane campus was the playground for many of Basso's immature pranks. These ranged from nailing professors' erasers to the floor to arranging a jazz serenade to be played underneath the Dean's window. Though not a favorite student with his professors, Basso became tremendously popular with his fellow students when, in midwinter, out of sheer ribaldry, he stripped to his shorts and dove into the Audubon Park lagoon. Although Charles Dufour, Basso's accomplice and friend, boasted that he and Basso were finally expelled from college, Basso claimed that he dropped out voluntarily because he could not picture himself a lawyer. In a newspaper article of 1954, he blamed New Orleans for his renouncing the law: with the city being such "a social place," Basso was convinced that something "like the law" was "apt to get in the way."[7]

Already during his law school semesters, Basso had traded in his lec-

---

5. Hamilton Basso, "A Momentary Digression," Typescript in Hamilton Basso Collection, Beinecke Library, Yale University, n.p.; Basso, *Cinnamon Seed* (New York, 1934), 6–7.

6. The law program already started at the undergraduate level.

7. Hamilton Basso, *New York Herald Tribune Book Review*, October 24, 1954, p. 4.

tures for the smoke-filled rooms of New Orleans' literary community. In the French Quarter, then still known as a prostitution quarter, the Louisiana writer Lyle Saxon had started a literary salon as early as 1919. Saxon predicted that "in the trail of artists," who had already settled there in the war years, "would come the writers and soon we would boast of our own Place D'Armes as New York does her Washington Square." By 1922, Saxon's prediction had come true. The Quarter saw the opening of photographers' studios and bohemian tearooms, and one year earlier, John McClure, Julius Weis Friend, and Albert Goldstein had founded the *Double Dealer*. Attracting many artists for whom Paris was too far and Greenwich Village too expensive, New Orleans offered a reasonable alternative. Depicting the city as a "Creole version of the Left Bank," Basso was to write many years after he had left the Big Easy, "If I never much hankered after Paris in the 1920s it was because . . . I had Paris in my own backyard."[8]

James Feibleman, one year younger than Basso, also frequented the *Double Dealer* hangouts and described the city as a "literary center," where despite Prohibition, "liquor was cheap and plentiful"; with its "sensually pleasant and socially tolerant atmosphere," the Quarter formed an ideal enclave for bohemians and hangers-on.[9]

Regardless of and because of the Quarter's derelict state, the neighborhood had a captivating charm that Sherwood Anderson, one of the older and more established writers at the *Double Dealer*, noted in his story "A Meeting South": "We walked slowly . . . through many streets of the Old Town. Negro women laughing all around us in the dusk, shadows playing over old buildings, children with their shrill cries dodging in and out of hallways. . . . Families were sitting down to dinner within full sight of the street—all doors and windows open. A man and his wife quarreled in Italian. In a patio back of an old building a Negress sang a French song."[10]

8. Cathy Chance Harvey, "Lyle Saxon: A Portrait in Letters, 1917–1945" (Ph.D. dissertation, Tulane University, 1980), 71; Hamilton Basso, "William Faulkner, Man and Writer," *Saturday Review,* July 28, 1962, p. 11.

9. James Feibleman, *The Way of Man: An Autobiography* (New York, 1952), 271–72.

10. Sherwood Anderson, "A Meeting South," in *The World from Jackson Square: A New Orleans Reader,* ed. Etolia S. Basso (New York, 1943), 345.

Site of the Pelican Book Shop at 407 Royal Street, where Hamilton Basso used to gather with friends from the *Double Dealer* group; now occupied by Raymond H. Weill Co., dealer in rare stamps
Courtesy Raymond H. Weill

Anderson's account shows that New Orleans bore then and still bears today more resemblance to a Mediterranean city than an American or southern city. Moreover, one is struck by the scene's easygoing atmosphere. This was also a feature of the *Double Dealer* group; despite the editors' resolute literary ambitions, the magazine was not averse to an element of fun, or as the editors wrote in their first issue, "A Skit, a jest, a jingle, making no pretense to the name of literature, is . . . a more honorable display of ink than a literary failure." Basso emphasized the *Double Dealer*'s relaxed stance: "We were not a literary clique, we were not a movement, and God knows we were not a school. . . . [W]hat held us together was a mutual friendliness and goodwill."[11] It was in this spirit also that the group gathered after closing hours at the Pelican Book Shop on Royal Street. The shades would be drawn, wine produced, and sitting down with a salami and a hunk of bread, the group would have their "tea." "It was a happy hour most of all and not, as we would perhaps be ready to believe, an intellectual hour."[12]

Despite the apparent frivolity of these *Double Dealer* impressions, one should not underestimate the importance of this publication. Fred Hobson claims that southern magazines like the *Double Dealer* and the Richmond *Reviewer* emerged as important rebuttals to H. L. Mencken's invective against the South as a "Sahara of the Bozart." In reply to Mencken's Dixie-bashing, the *Double Dealer* editors avowed that the South did have a culture, and they endowed their efforts with a considerable degree of self-importance by subtitling the *Double Dealer* a "National Magazine of the South." In their repudiation of certain southern stigmas, they further stated that it was "high time . . . for some doughty, clear-visioned pen man to emerge from the sodden marshes of Southern literature." Being "sick to death of the treacly sentimentalities with which our well-intentioned lady fiction-eers regale us," the editors claimed that the old traditions and the Confederacy should no longer be on southerners' minds: "A storied

11. *Double Dealer,* I (March, 1921), 83; Basso, "William Faulkner," 11.

12. Etolia S. Basso, interview with the author, January 3, 1991, Tempe, Arizona. Royal Street would later be described by Basso as a "good part of town. It was old and broken-down and not even the imitation artists and Bohemians could spoil it. They had done their best to spoil it but somehow or other . . . the Quarter managed to absorb all its invaders and come off relatively unscarred" (Basso, *Days Before Lent,* 59).

realm of dreams, lassitude, pleasure, chivalry and the Nigger no longer exists."[13]

It is important to realize that the *Double Dealer* view influenced Basso when he had only begun to form his opinions of southern literature. Accordingly, Basso clearly echoes the *Double Dealer* when he writes that he wants to depart from Dixie's "romantic . . . emotionalism" and tell about a South that was to be different from Julia Peterkin's and Lyle Saxon's "pretty wallpaper" versions. In the same vein was his continued insistence on wanting to capture the "essential reality of the South" and his desire "to get rid of all the old sentimental truck and explain, by using facts instead of poetry, what has happened here in the South and why this romantic conception is so untrue" and go back to the rhetoric and founding principles of the magazine. Besides leaving a mark on Basso's early poetics, the *Double Dealer* also was a catalyst in the southern renascence. Although the magazine was constantly short of funds and struggled to survive, Hobson points out that the magazine "urged a critical examination of Southern tradition, and in doing so infused young writers centered in New Orleans (including Faulkner) with a sense of excitement and new purpose concerning the possibilities of Southern literature." Despite the magazine's initial regional orientation, by 1922 it had turned to the national scene and in tune with the modernist *Zeitgeist* started to publish experimental fiction by such writers as Faulkner, Hemingway, Jean Toomer, and Thornton Wilder. Basso thought the opportunity to experiment one of the merits of this little magazine.[14] His own inclination toward experimentation, especially noticeable in his early work and first novel, may have stemmed from the *Double Dealer*, too.

Frances Bowen Durrett ranks the magazine as "one of the most important organs for the development of struggling artists during the period [of the] Southern literary renascence." She has calculated that of the 293 contributors to the *Double Dealer*, 55 were sufficiently prominent to make *Who's Who in America* thirty years after the magazine had first

13. Fred Hobson, *Serpent in Eden* (Chapel Hill, 1974), 33–56; *Double Dealer*, I (June, 1921), 2.

14. Hamilton Basso to Maxwell Perkins, February 1, 1930, November 30, 1931, August 13, 1932, Scribner's Archives, Firestone Library, Princeton University; Fred Hobson, *Serpent in Eden*, 48; Hamilton Basso, letter to Frances Bowen Durrett, July 20, 1952, in Basso Collection, Beinecke Library.

been published. Enticing both established and would-be writers, the *Double Dealer* was, in Basso's words, "fun," and "something to be in on. . . . It was a kind of cross between student days in Paris in the 1890's, and the Jazz age of the U.S. in the 1920's."[15]

Bowen Durrett places Sherwood Anderson at the center of the magazine and draws a rather flattering portrait of him: "His hospitality was without bounds, as was also his lack of social discrimination. No one was too dull or too conceited or too undesirable to be interesting. He was never hurried but listened endlessly to anyone who sought him out, and demonstrated a genius for smoothing out human snarls." Anderson's contemporaries give a somewhat different picture. William Spratling, at the time a young architecture professor at Tulane, writes how Anderson was not at all interested in a young Mississippi "squirt" named William Faulkner. Although Faulkner and Anderson would largely resolve their initial and mutually felt animosity, the two would remain at odds with each other, especially when either one wanted to be the center of attention: Spratling tells us that Anderson could not stand it when Faulkner "spoke out of turn or distracted Sherwood's listeners."[16]

Anderson's vanity is also apparent in an anecdote told by Spratling, who, together with William Faulkner, offered Anderson a little book of caricatures, *Sherwood Anderson and Other Famous Creoles* (1926):

> [Spratling] made the drawings of all the "artful and crafty ones" in our group, Faulkner did the editing. We paid to have this thin little book of caricature—a spoof at Sherwood—printed. . . . Though certainly not literature, it may now be considered a sort of mirror of our scene in New Orleans.
>
> When it arrived from the press, we very proudly visited Sherwood that evening and handed him his copy. He turned it over, looking inside, scowled and said, "I don't think it's very funny." Sherwood was taking himself very seriously at that time. He had recently been referred to by a critic as the "Dean of American Literature."

15. Frances Bowen Durrett, "The New Orleans *Double Dealer*," in *Reality and Myth: Essays in American Literature*, ed. William E. Walker and Robert L. Welker (Nashville, 1964), 212; Basso to Durrett, July 20, 1952, in Basso Collection, Beinecke Library.

16. Durrett, "The New Orleans *Double Dealer*," 222–23; William Spratling, *File on Spratling: An Autobiography* (Boston, 1967), 22.

Hamilton Basso dancing the Charleston with the Muse,
from *Sherwood Anderson and Other Famous Creoles*, 1926

Among the rather benign caricatures is a dazzling portrait of Hamilton Basso dancing the Charleston with the Muse. The picture's caption reads: "A happy conception of the artist, the significance of which has slipped his mind in the interval. Picture has to do with superiority of agile heels over the keenest brain in captivating that elusive female, success."[17] Clearly, this alludes to Basso's dancing talent as well as to his serious literary ambitions.

Hamilton Basso's relationship with Sherwood Anderson seems to have been a trifle ambivalent, too. As one of the youngest members of the

17. Spratling, *File*, 22, 28–29; *Sherwood Anderson and Other Famous Creoles*, ed. William Faulkner and William Spratling (New Orleans, 1926), n.p.

Double Dealer group, Basso naturally deferred to the peremptory personality of Anderson, at whose feet he literally liked to sit. Consequently, in Basso's early career, he says rather praiseworthy things about Anderson. Also, in his correspondence with the *Winesburg, Ohio,* author, he envisioned Anderson to be the model leader of an "Intellectual Party" and revealed endearingly: "I couldn't be more deeply devoted to you. . . . I owe you a debt that I can never even hope to repay."[18]

In later years Basso became an unrelenting critic of the former dean of American letters: in musing on how some writers become like the characters they create, Basso described Anderson as "one of those half-articulate, muggy-minded people that turn up in Winesburg." He deprecated his former mentor further in a letter to Elizabeth Nowell, in which he attributed a quarrel Thomas Wolfe and Anderson had had in the past to Anderson's "streak of malice," which occasionally turned him into a "trouble-maker." Yet in the same letter, he admitted squarely that Anderson "too is dead now, and was kind of generous to me back in the old days in New Orleans, and I wouldn't want to injure him in any way. The blunt truth of the matter is that all literary men are apt to be extremely disagreeable at times, and that's all there is to it."[19]

Basso was also relatively close to Faulkner. They were first introduced in 1924, when he and Faulkner were dinner guests of the Andersons. What he remembered best about that evening was not only Faulkner's gentlemanliness, which surfaced in his "beautiful manners, his soft speech," and "his controlled intensity," but also his not-so-gentlemanly "astonishing capacity for hard drink." Although neither writer had published any major work at this point, Basso felt on account of his young age that, in Faulkner's company, he had been "admitted to the ball park by mistake." He felt particularly wet behind the ears when he discussed literature with Faulkner: whereas Faulkner had most of the Modernists (Verlaine, Eliot, Pound, and Joyce) under his belt, Basso was still struggling with Conrad and Melville. He also noticed the differences in their southern background: Basso identified with what he called a Mediterranean, Catholic, and European tradition, whereas Faulkner's hinterland

18. Hamilton Basso to Sherwood Anderson, August 6, 1931, and undated letter, in Sherwood Anderson Collection, Newberry Library, Chicago.

19. Hamilton Basso, notes for a *New Yorker* profile on Eugene O'Neill, Typescript, September 7, 1947, in Basso Collection, Beinecke Library; Hamilton Basso to Elizabeth Nowell, April 27, 1949, in Basso Collection, Beinecke Library.

was "much less diluted, *sui generis* Anglo-Saxon, Protestant, and, as it were, more land-locked, turned inward upon itself." This difference triggered many a conversation between the two writers, who would sometimes go for long walks on the wharves. Their friendship intensified when they went flying together with the Gates Flying Circus. This circus of reckless aviators, flying rickety planes, was a novelty in town. Since Basso was then a young feature writer on the New Orleans *Times-Picayune* and was therefore considered "the least expensive" and most "expendable" of the paper's journalists, he was sent by his city editor to report on the spectacle. Faulkner, who had a lifelong fascination with aviation, accompanied Basso on these flights. Basso observed later that "nobody *else* in our crowd had gone looping-the-loop in a bucket seat and open cockpit over the Mississippi River."[20]

When Faulkner died in 1962, Basso wrote a sympathetic obituary in the *Saturday Review.* In the piece he recalled their New Orleans days and admitted that Faulkner's *oeuvre* was too complex for him; he attributed this complexity to Faulkner's Modernist techniques and mythologizing of the South, which was not, in Basso's eyes, the South but "Faulkner's vision of the South. . . . Those who read him as a 'realistic' novelist might just as well read Dante as a Baedeker to the nether regions and Milton as a Michelin going in the opposite direction."[21] Notwithstanding this droll criticism, he respected Faulkner's work highly, and whereas his praise for Anderson gradually disappeared over the years, his admiration for Faulkner continued to grow.

A last but not unimportant contact was Lyle Saxon. Basso's senior by thirteen years, Saxon was, like Anderson, a kind of father figure for young and struggling artists. Proof of this can be found in a letter in which Basso thanked Saxon for helping his brother-in-law, the painter John McCrady: "Your belief in his stuff has helped him immensely—just as your belief, and your great encouragement, have always helped me."[22] Cathy Chance Harvey claims that Basso was a "sad kind of person" and that Saxon would "keep him bucked up."[23] Although we should probably

---

20. Basso, "William Faulkner," 11, 12.

21. *Ibid.,* 13.

22. Hamilton Basso to Lyle Saxon, November 29, 1937, in Lyle Saxon Collection, Howard-Tilton Memorial Library, Tulane University.

23. Harvey, "Lyle Saxon," 138. Etolia Basso disagrees with this and believes that Saxon was less influential than Harvey claims.

question Harvey's assumption that Saxon kept Basso "bucked up long after he left Louisiana," it is true that Saxon's support was generous and never wavered. In a *Herald Tribune* book review of Basso's *Courthouse Square* (1936), Saxon was even so magnanimous as to argue that the novel placed Basso "among the significant writers of the South" and incorporated "the fine fulfillment of the promise given in his earlier books." Conversely, Saxon's benevolence was not always reciprocated by Basso; when it was his turn to write a complimentary review of Saxon's only novel, *Children of Strangers* (1937), Basso produced a very flat-sounding piece in which he made fun of Saxon's inside knowledge of Louisiana: "Mr. Lyle Saxon . . . knows more about Louisiana than many people know about their apartments." Although Basso apologized for the review by writing a very ingratiating letter in which he told Saxon that the *New Republic* had cut one-third of the review without notifying him, one may question Basso's sincerity; not only did he dislike Saxon's flighty plantation idylls, he was not very forthcoming either when he described Saxon to Thomas Wolfe as "a sort of the Ward McAllister of the New Orleans intellectual circles and not such a bad guy if you don't expect too much: maybe a little old ladyish." Remarkably, after having visited Saxon, Wolfe used Basso's words in his notebook: "An old lady—not a phony."[24]

Basso's ambivalence may be ascribed to Saxon's position as a relative outsider to the *Double Dealer* circle. Although the group feigned a spirit of camaraderie and mutual encouragement, which Faulkner described as a fellowship of art and Oliver LaFarge endorsed with his claim that "when one of us achieved anything at all, however slight, the others were delighted and I think everyone took new courage," Harvey insists that there was no such bonding and that the formation of cliques of those who came from New Orleans and those who came from out of town was inevitable: "The inner circle of the *Double Dealer,* composed of members of established New Orleans families, was not always open to outsiders. For example, although Saxon served on the magazine's staff for seven months, he was not close to founder Julius Friend."[25]

24. Lyle Saxon, "Uneasy Blood in Their Veins," *New York Herald Tribune Book Review,* November 1, 1936, p. 8; Hamilton Basso, "Bayou People," *New Republic,* September 1, 1937, p. 108; Hamilton Basso to Thomas Wolfe, October 20, 1936, in William Wisdom Collection, Houghton Library, Harvard University; Harvey, "Lyle Saxon," 358.

25. Harvey, "Lyle Saxon," 114.

Despite the good times Basso had in New Orleans, he understood that the Crescent City was by no means the literary mecca of the United States. He knew that if he wanted to become a serious writer he should either go to Paris and blend in with the expatriate crowd while trying to get published in one of the little magazines issued from the Left Bank or rent a garret in the heart of Greenwich Village and try to interest a publisher. Having chosen the latter course, Basso departed for New York on June 7, 1926. Apparently, he had a job lined up for him at a New York newspaper, the *Sun,* which had been arranged by Lyle Saxon. But his correspondence with Anderson shows that he was almost constantly without work. Experiencing the metropolis as "an oyster" that to his "hurt astonishment wouldn't open," Basso returned to New Orleans in winter, 1926.[26]

Of his return there are no actual records, but his wife, Etolia Basso, remembers that he came home depressed and disappointed. Edmund Wilson must have sensed his friend's discomfort as he responded to one of Basso's letters with the remark, "I can see how New Orleans would get on your nerves, but would give anything to be able to go there myself."[27] The best impression of Basso's feelings upon his return home is provided by an insightful letter he sent to former *Double Dealer* member Eugene Jolas.[28] Besides being a sharp critique of the gentrification of the Quarter, the letter conveys a sense of alienation that seems typical of someone who has lost touch with his hometown. Dismayed by the commercialization of the Quarter, Basso felt weaned from his former habitat. He was especially repulsed by the clique of artists, who, drawn by the reputation of the fading *Double Dealer,* sat around in bookshops to swap ideas: "They make me feel as though I ought to hurry home and take a bath," Basso tells Jolas. Repelled by any form of artistic exhibitionism, he was also highly unassuming about his own literary ambitions. In challenging John McClure, who defended the poet John Fineran on account of his young age, Basso commented that youth should never be "an excuse for poor poetry." He added that though he himself felt the process of youth "very

26. "Hamilton Basso," *Wilson Library Bulletin,* XIV (October, 1939), 186.

27. Etolia S. Basso, interview with the author, May 4, 1992, Tempe, Arizona; Edmund Wilson to Hamilton Basso, January 25, 1927, in *Letters on Literature and Politics, 1912–1972,* ed. Elena Wilson (London, 1977), 132–33.

28. After receiving the letter, Jolas published it in his little magazine, *transition.* Hamilton Basso, "New Orleans Letter," *transition* (February, 1929), 149–50.

keenly," he would "vomit" if anybody told him that he was "a promising young writer." Basso's overall disappointment should be attributed to the Quarter's changing climate, for like Basso, Roark Bradford observed in a letter to Lyle Saxon that "too many country boys and girls are coming in to be Bohemians and immorality lacks that calm, professional dignity it held in the corrupt era prior to 1927."[29]

Shortly after Basso returned from New York City, he was hired again by the *Times-Picayune*. Working most of his shifts at night, he tried to do some serious writing of his own during the day. But his night shifts and busy social life were not very conducive to writing novels; Basso needed a room of his own in order to get pen to paper, and in a letter to a friend, he inquired after a cabin in the Louisiana countryside. Looking forward to having time off and finishing a novel he had been working on since 1926, Basso joked that his sociable temperament was not a suitable foundation for the isolation a writer has to endure: "I am essentially a creature of civilization, with a penchant for debutantes or part debutantes who smell nice, jazz, booze and all the other awful, awful vices."[30] In the same letter, Basso expected that by the summertime he would have saved enough money "to bide off a year or so." This plan never materialized; *Relics and Angels* (1929), Basso's debut novel, was not completed in the Louisiana countryside but was finished on Grande Isle in 1928. Basso's loitering in New Orleans in 1927 and 1928 could best be explained by his falling in love with Etolia Simmons.

Ham and Etolia, or Toto, as she was called, had both attended Tulane but knew each other only vaguely from parties. This changed when Toto started working for the Pelican Book Shop. According to Toto, she and Ham became friends very gradually; although she was attracted to his good looks, white linen suits, and maroon ties, romance was slow to unfold. However, when Ham returned from New York, they met again and "became very good friends."

Toto was the only daughter of a well-to-do St. Louis family. Her father, Roger Simmons, became a national hero after having witnessed the October Revolution and surviving a Moscow prison sentence. On returning to the United States in 1918, he and his family moved to New Orleans, where he prospered in the lumber business. Etolia attended Sophie

29. *Ibid.*, 150; Harvey, "Lyle Saxon," 208.
30. Hamilton Basso to Eugene Matrange, April 22, 1927, in Basso Collection, Tulane University.

Newcomb, the women's college at Tulane, and was graduated in 1926, the year that Basso dropped out. The Tulane yearbooks show her to have been a young woman active in many clubs and sports events. Although Etolia denies having been a sought-after beauty, Malcolm Cowley has written that Basso stole her away "from twenty or thirty young lawyers and newspapermen who had the same glint in their eyes." He finally proposed to her during a romantic dinner at Galatoire's, one of New Orleans' famous restaurants. Toto's parents were not pleased with the prospect of giving away their daughter to a struggling young writer, or as Toto herself remembered in her customary deadpan manner: "They did not think much of it."[31]

The two got married in the summer of 1930. Because Ham was Catholic and Toto Protestant, they avoided the ado of New Orleans and chose the quiet North Carolina countryside for their wedding. The ceremony was held in the beautiful garden of Toto's friends, Mr. and Mrs. Henry Carriere. The announcement in the *Times-Picayune*, stating that Ham and Toto's wedding was going to be "one of the very interesting out-of-town nuptials of the early summer," indicates that they were a popular New Orleans couple. As for the wedding itself, when the bishop arrived—on horseback—to have the couple exchange their vows in the open air, Toto may have wondered what she was getting herself into. Although her husband had taken a job as a copywriter with a New Orleans advertising agency, he really wanted to become a full-time novelist.

After the wedding, the Bassos moved back to New Orleans, where Ham tried to write a new book as well as find another publisher. Although Macaulay, the publisher of his first novel, was ready to take on another manuscript, Basso was shopping around, sending outlines, ideas, and full stories to various publishers. As early as 1927 he had already approached Maxwell Perkins, the famous editor of F. Scott Fitzgerald, Ernest Hemingway, and—supremely—Thomas Wolfe. In a letter of February 1, 1930, Basso informed Perkins that he was writing a novel, which in typical *Double Dealer* fashion would be a radical departure from antebellum myths and what Basso perceived as southern "emotionalism." In a subsequent letter Basso hinted to Perkins that he had broken with Macaulay because he was tired of "laying in the same bed with

---

31. Malcolm Cowley, notes for eulogy on Basso, in Malcolm Cowley Collection, Newberry Library, Chicago; Etolia S. Basso, interview, January 16, 1992, Tempe.

Peggy Joyce etc." He casually mentioned that he had "chunked the manuscript of a perfectly lousy novel into the river"; to Perkins' puzzled response Basso exclaimed, "What the hell! There are too many incompetents slinging ink."[32]

Following Edmund Wilson's advice "to keep at it, in spite of hell," Basso then sent Perkins the manuscript of another novel with the working title "A Room in the Sky." At the time, Basso worried that he would be unable to publish anything after the meager success of *Relics and Angels*. Perkins' reply was painfully short but honest: "In spite of its unusual talent cannot think publication practicable. Deeply sorry."[33] With the Depression worsening, Perkins had to be very careful about what he published, selective and parsimonious. As for Basso, besides it being difficult to get a foot in the door at Scribner's or one of the other New York publishing houses, his full-time job as copywriter at Fitzgerald Advertising Agency distracted him from doing any substantial literary work.

In the meantime, the Depression had cast its long shadow over the South. Basso personally felt the sting of the Depression when in 1931 he was fired by Fitzgerald. Having been the last man in, he was the first man out, and even though he had intended to leave the company anyway, his forced departure came a year too early. He had resented the advertising world of soups, soaps, and sodas, but the job gave him financial security plus the opportunity to save money for the period when he worked as a full-time freelance writer. With the little savings they had, the Bassos decided to leave New Orleans and settle in the North Carolina mountains. They left the city in a melancholy mood. Both of them had grown up in the Big Easy, and both had known very pleasant times in the French Quarter. Basso evidently felt, however, that he needed to leave: by 1931, he was denigrating New Orleans as a "provincial backwater."[34]

Basso would ultimately develop a love-hate relationship with his hometown: although he had outgrown New Orleans and consequently had a hard time going back, the city remained for him "the last place in the South where people know how to have fun. The rest of the South,"

32. Hamilton Basso to Maxwell Perkins, February 1, 1930, in Scribner's Archives; Hamilton Basso to Maxwell Perkins, May 17, 1930, in Scribner's Archives.

33. Edmund Wilson to Hamilton Basso, May 9, 1929, in *Letters on Literature and Politics*, ed. Wilson, 173; Maxwell Perkins to Hamilton Basso, June 3, 1931, in Scribner's Archives.

34. Hamilton Basso to Sherwood Anderson, June 19, 1931, in Scribner's Archives.

Basso wrote in a letter to Malcolm Cowley, "is too joylessly Anglo-Saxon." It is perhaps not so surprising that Basso projected his mixed feelings onto the heroes in his novels. A return home, whether it was his own or Beauregard's or David Barondess', always triggered feelings of alienation and nostalgia. And although Basso left New Orleans permanently in 1932, it was emotionally difficult for him to sever all ties. Not until the end of his life, after he had written his last novel dealing with the South, did Basso finally sever his ties with the city of his birth. Sitting on deck of a ship that was to take him from New Orleans to Tahiti in 1958, he wrote in his diary:

> I suspect I have used up my sentiment for and about New Orleans: I *could* go home again, but I doubt that I could stand it for long: it's the provincialism, it's the provincial aspirations—like so many of its sister cities in the United States, New Orleans won't be minor league—which was its charm and its appeal. I didn't even much enjoy walking in the French Quarter this time, though that may have been because of the weather. I don't think so, however. It could be that I have used up the last of my memories, and so am free of them—in one way or another, one eventually shakes loose.[35]

35. Hamilton Basso to Malcolm Cowley, April 29, 1940, in Cowley Collection; Hamilton Basso, "Tahiti Diary," Typescript, entry dated November 6, 1958, in Basso Collection, Beinecke Library.

Lillian Hellman
By permission of the Billy Rose Theatre Collection,
New York Public Library for the Performing Arts,
Astor, Lenox and Tilden Foundations

Fillalloo Bird of New Orleans:
Lillian Hellman

MAUREEN RYAN

"What becomes a legend most?" asked the mid-1970s magazine advertisements that featured female celebrities glamorously swathed in Blackgama mink coats. It was no coincidence that one of the more memorable of those ads featured a seventy-year-old Lillian Hellman posed insouciantly in mink; by then, late in her life, Hellman—the stalwart, flamboyant playwright and memoirist whose life spanned much of this century; the feisty moralist who, at age seventy-five, filed a defamation suit against fellow writer Mary McCarthy because she called Hellman a liar on the *Dick Cavett Show*—was indeed a legend.

Lillian Hellman was very much ahead of her time. A successful playwright in an era when women in the theater were usually confined to dressing rooms and prosceniums. A political activist who faced down the House Committee on Un-American Activities with her famous refusal to testify against her friends: "I cannot and will not cut my conscience to fit this year's fashions." A woman whose peripatetic lifestyle took her to Hollywood, Moscow, New York City, and Pleasantville, New York, where she lived in a tempestuous and unconventional long-term relationship with fellow writer Dashiell Hammett.

Hellman was forthright and unsentimental, as her eight uncompromising plays on themes like greed and betrayal and self-delusion deftly demonstrate. Throughout her work and in her life, she cast a keen and often critical eye on politics, the theater, her personal relationships—and her past: "I have no love for the past, written or remembered," she asserted. "To hell with all that happened once upon a time."[1] And yet, dismiss it as she might, Hellman's past—her southern family, her childhood in New Orleans, her evolving self—emerges again and again (and, as she aged, increasingly) throughout her work.

Hellman was born in 1905 in New Orleans to a struggling Jewish businessman and his wife. She would later immortalize her mother's wealthy Alabama family as the rapacious Hubbards in her plays *The Little Foxes* and *Another Part of the Forest*. For the first six years of her life, Hellman lived with her parents and her father's two older sisters in her aunts' boardinghouse on Prytania Street near the Garden District in New Orleans. In her later life, in interviews and in her autobiographical books (*An Unfinished Woman, Pentimento,* and the fictionalized *Maybe*), she remembered with fondness her early years in the indolent, cosmopolitan city that has entranced so many American writers. She recalls shopping with one of her aunts in the French Market for ingredients for the rich Creole dishes that she would cook throughout her life. She describes the fig tree in the yard that became the private refuge of an only child in a house full of adults. And she offers early evidence of the fascination with character that would make her such a compelling writer. "I was crazy about other people's lives," she noted about the colorful boardinghouse. "I guess I was the only one who ever listened to the guests, and they talked to me for hours."[2]

Hellman lived in New Orleans only during her early childhood,

1. Lillian Hellman, "On Reading Again," in *Three* (Boston, 1979), 5.
2. "A Successful Playwright Recalls Her Childhood in New Orleans," New Orleans *Times-Picayune*, April 19, 1959, p. 29.

The Hellman boardinghouse at 1716 Prytania Street
Photo by Maureen Ryan

though after her family's move to New York in 1911 she returned throughout her adolescence to visit her aunts for half of every year (with a deleterious effect on her education). In her adulthood she acknowledged that she had no "right" to claim southernness; "but," she asserted, "I suppose most Southerners, people who grew up in the South, still consider themselves Southern. . . . I came from a family of Southerners. . . . I came from a family, on both sides, who had been Southerners for a great many generations." The South, Hellman wrote in *Pentimento* in 1973, is "home to me still."[3]

There is no question but that her early years in New Orleans had a lingering influence on Hellman's life and work. Certainly, her plays—the Hubbard plays; *The Autumn Garden,* set in a summer resort on the Mississippi Gulf Coast; and *Toys in the Attic,* her last original play (an adaptation followed), about a brother who returns to the New Orleans boardinghouse of his two elder sisters—and also the fact that each of the many

3. Stephanie de Pue, "Lillian Hellman: She Never Turns Down an Adventure," in *Conversations with Lillian Hellman,* ed. Jackson R. Bryer (Jackson, Miss., 1986), 184; Lillian Hellman, *Pentimento* (Boston, 1973), 94.

stories of childhood in her memoirs is a memory of New Orleans (never New York) attest to the abiding impact of the city and the South on Hellman, both as a woman and as an artist. What is remarkable about the importance of New Orleans in her work is the degree to which her childhood, and her attitudes about her childhood, reflect the playwright's unique sensibility: her refusal to romanticize herself and her themes, her unwavering commitment to personal courage and fundamental values, and her ambivalence about her own time and the world around her.

Acknowledging that all writers use their own pasts for material, Hellman cautioned against a sentimental attitude toward childhood: "Most childhoods are a mixture of happiness and unhappiness just like the rest of life." She commented frequently on her unusual, bifurcated adolescence, the shuttling back and forth between New York and New Orleans. Richard Poirier, in his introduction to *Three* (the single-volume reprinting of *An Unfinished Woman, Pentimento,* and *Scoundrel Time*), conjectures that Hellman's associative structure in her memoirs illustrates "that capacity for movement back and forth which she learned as a young child. . . . In a child so questing and questioning and anxious for love, the unsettling and resettling also nurtured a genius, essential to the kind of writer she was to become, for seeing persons and places in their context and within the complex changes wrought by the passage of time and geographic separations."[4] Indeed, Hellman's vision of the world— and her childhood in New Orleans—was always complex, relative, and ambivalent.

In December, 1963, *Ladies' Home Journal* featured a short article by Hellman entitled "Sophronia's Grandson Goes to Washington," her account of the August civil rights march on Washington, which the editors commissioned, they say in a short introduction to the piece, because they wanted the insights of an "artist . . . [and] along with recollections of a New Orleans girlhood, Miss Hellman brought to the march the clear eye of a trained observer, the sensitivity and skill of one of America's major dramatists, and the *tempered affection for the South* that characterizes her work in such plays as *The Little Foxes, Another Part of the Forest,* and *Toys in the Attic.*" As Hellman begins the essay, she muses about Sophronia, her beloved childhood nurse, and "realize[s] again how deep were my roots in the South, how I had loved it and not loved it." No

---

4. "A Successful Playwright," 29; Richard Poirier, Introduction to *Three*, xiii–xiv.

Quentin Compson, Hellman understands and admits her ambivalence about her early years in the South. Whereas scholars have noted that her Jewishness is hardly mentioned in her plays and memoirs, Hellman acknowledges that she is "very conscious" of her Jewish heritage; and although she observes that "New Orleans Jews, just as New Orleans people, were a breed apart," she also notes that "New Orleans had a live-and-let-live quality about it. That was rare in the South."[5]

Part New Yorker, part New Orleanian; Jewish in a Protestant society; a bright only child; a white child raised in part by black women; physically unattractive by conventional standards in a society that prized female beauty, Lillian Hellman was formed by contradictions. No wonder she pronounced of her earliest home that "it's a funny city to grow up in. . . . New Orleans does odd things to people. It did odd things to me too."[6] We can only be grateful, because her "oddness," in part created and nurtured by her lifelong fascination with the city of New Orleans, is the source of her powerful drama and memoirs.

Lillian Hellman was first and perhaps foremost a dramatist. Often acknowledged as America's premiere woman playwright (a label that she understandably disliked),[7] she enjoyed a successful career in the theater for thirty years, beginning with the popular and critical acclaim for her first, daring play, *The Children's Hour* (1934), and continuing through the autobiographical *Toys in the Attic* (1960). And as the Royal Shakespeare Company's 1994 production of *The Children's Hour* indicates, Hellman's plays continue to speak to contemporary audiences. Lillian Hellman remains an important American playwright. In a sense, in her dramatic work Hellman moved ever closer to New Orleans and her childhood with her beloved aunts; from the New England setting of *Children's Hour*, to the Alabama entrepreneurs of *The Little Foxes* and *Another Part of the Forest* in 1939 and 1946, to the Gulf Coast summer house of *The Autumn Garden* (1951), and finally to the New Orleans boardinghouse of *Toys in the Attic* and the gentle, faded, but dignified New Orleans

5. Lillian Hellman, "Sophronia's Grandson Goes to Washington," *Ladies' Home Journal,* LXXX (December, 1963), 78 (emphasis mine); Christine Doudna, "A Still Unfinished Woman: A Conversation with Lillian Hellman," in *Conversations with Lillian Hellman,* ed. Bryer, 196–97.

6. Peter Feibleman, *Lilly: Reminiscences of Lillian Hellman* (New York, 1988), 23.

7. William Wright, *Lillian Hellman: The Image, the Woman* (New York, 1986), 98.

people who contrast so dramatically with the treacherous Hubbards. Yet Hellman's early life and the values that she learned from her years in New Orleans resonate throughout all of her plays.

W. Kenneth Holditch, in an essay on Lillian Hellman as a southern playwright, demonstrates how "Hellman's work is indelibly marked by the specific place of her origin." He characterizes as distinctly southern Hellman's paradoxical but "abiding conviction" of both "the natural depravity of human beings" and "the virtues often exhibited in the aristocratic class of society." He identifies other peculiarly southern attitudes in Hellman's plays: her concern for ecology and the land; her "sense of one's obligations to family, society, and race; a devotion to family pride, which includes the motif of inheritance; and a conviction that lost causes may somehow function beneficially in forging character." Holditch discusses the influence of the South, including New Orleans, in Hellman's settings, her characters, and her use of language. His case for classifying Hellman as a "southern" playwright is convincing. Yet as Holditch notes, Hellman's only New Orleans play, *Toys in the Attic*, seems less southern than the Hubbard plays, because in her final two original plays, *Toys* and *Autumn Garden*, Hellman moves to "a consideration of more private, intimate concerns."[8]

Indeed, *Toys in the Attic*, Hellman's dramatic portrait of two strong-willed, aging spinster sisters and their psychologically complex (today we would say "dysfunctional") relationship with their charming, ne'er-do-well younger brother, seems to have marked the turn of Hellman's attentions inward and homeward. Her next original work was the acclaimed 1969 memoir *An Unfinished Woman*. Throughout this and her subsequent autobiographical writing, Hellman returns again and again to her early years with her extended family in the Crescent City.

Hellman begins *An Unfinished Woman* with her mother's family, but she immediately declares that her "first love" was for her "free, generous, funny" father and his sisters, and for their boardinghouse, her "first and most beloved home." Her early years and her adolescent extended visits to New Orleans were, Hellman asserts, "always the best times of my life." Indeed, her affection for daily life at the boardinghouse—skipping school for long, leisurely days of reading in the fig tree that clearly sym-

8. W. Kenneth Holditch, "Another Part of the Country: Lillian Hellman as Southern Playwright," *Southern Quarterly*, XXV (Spring, 1987), 16, 17, 34.

bolizes a young girl's private self; buying old books in the French Quarter with her Aunt Hannah; learning from Aunt Jenny to cook New Orleans food—is palpable, not only throughout *An Unfinished Woman* but in *Pentimento* and *Maybe* as well. Always the dramatist, she offers her perceptions about her life—in *An Unfinished Woman* and even more notably in *Pentimento*'s "Book of Portraits"—through discrete episodes, describing memorable events through which the young Hellman learns lessons about herself and the world around her. In one long, complicated episode in *An Unfinished Woman,* Hellman runs away rather than admit her affection for an orphan boy, spends a night roaming the streets of the Vieux Carré, starts to menstruate, and is finally rescued by her father. From this surreal night she learns her "power" over her parents as well as the "more dangerous" lesson that "if you are willing to take the punishment, you are halfway through the battle." In the opening portrait of *Pentimento,* "Bethe," her story of a German relative who is sent to New Orleans for an arranged marriage and who teaches Hellman a lasting lesson about romantic love, Hellman interposes the mystery of her grandfather's notebooks, which she discovered at age sixteen at the boardinghouse and which she expected to receive when her aunts died. But when Hannah dies nearly thirty years later, the valise containing the notebooks mysteriously disappears. A perplexed Hellman contemplates this, Hannah's "only alien, unfriendly act," and wonders whether her beloved aunts perceived her, a writer, as "a different breed . . . a stranger."[9]

Memorable youthful events like these—memorable at least to a much older Lillian Hellman, who, throughout her autobiographical writing, cautions us and herself about the limitations of memory—instilled in the young writer-to-be the strong moral sensibility that characterizes her work. Yet always, in Hellman's memoirs as in her plays, the places and events are secondary to the characters. Perhaps Hellman turns increasingly to New Orleans in her introspective later writing because it was in New Orleans that she knew and loved the fascinating, powerful people who so influenced her life and her work: the aunts, Bethe, Willy, and her beloved Sophronia.

Sophronia, Hellman's childhood nurse, was, she writes, "the first and most certain love of my life." It is Sophronia to whom the adolescent

---

9. Lillian Hellman, *An Unfinished Woman* (Boston, 1969), 5, 10, 16, 29; Hellman, *Pentimento,* 16.

Lilly, age three, with her nurse, Sophronia
From the playbill of the Royal National Theatre, London, for The Children's Hour

Hellman runs on that difficult night in the Quarter as she struggles to understand her capacity for anger and her sexuality, Sophronia who instructs the young Lillian in stoicism and discretion when the child witnesses her father in the company of "a faded, sexy, giggly . . . lady boarder" from her aunts' boardinghouse. Sophronia's dignity and composure also taught Hellman of the injustice of racism and surely influenced her lifelong political activism. In her *Ladies' Home Journal* article, Hellman appends to her recognition of her ambivalent ties to the South her understanding that "so much of me had been molded by a Negro woman, and molded to last for good." Sophronia is undoubtedly the model for Coralee in *Another Part of the Forest* and, more obviously, for Addie, "the tall, nice-looking Negro woman" in *The Little Foxes*. Wise Addie, who dotes on Horace and Alexandra, and who knows that Regina is no woman to cross, is the moral center of Hellman's most famous play; she expresses the central theme of the play and obliquely explains its title (from the Song of Solomon) when she proclaims, "There are people who eat the earth and eat all the people on it like in the Bible with locusts. And other people who stand around and watch them eat it. Sometimes I think it ain't right to stand and watch them do it."[10]

Throughout her memoirs, Hellman recognizes and cherishes the influence of Sophronia on her life: "Oh, Sophronia," she writes at the end of *An Unfinished Woman*, "it's you I want back always. It's by you I still so often measure, guess, transmute, translate and act. What strange process made a little girl strain so hard to hear the few words that ever came, made the image of you, true or false, last a lifetime?"[11]

Much of Lillian Hellman was molded, too, by her beloved aunts, Jenny and Hannah, the sisters whose subtly rendered relationship is the most interesting aspect of *Toys in the Attic*. Hellman writes frequently and always lovingly of these southern ladies who "had lived doing the uncomplaining work of women brought up by middle-class intellectual parents who grew more educated as they grew poorer; going out to find any kind of work in a social class where that was a kind of disgrace . . . proud, cranky, married to each other; frightened of life with brave faces." Hannah, who held a job downtown, was the indulgent aunt who applauded her niece's childish wilfulness as "a mark of intelligence and

10. Hellman, *An Unfinished Woman,* 14, 15; Hellman, "Sophronia's Grandson," 79; Lillian Hellman, *The Little Foxes,* in *The Collected Plays* (Boston, 1972), 135, 182.
11. Hellman, *An Unfinished Woman,* 235–36.

Anna Revere, Jason Robards, and Maureen Stapleton in a scene from a 1960 production of
Toys in the Attic
*By permission of the Billy Rose Theatre Collection, New York Public Library for the Performing
Arts, Astor, Lenox and Tilden Foundations*

splendid, emerging character." Jenny, who ran the house, was "good-natured irritable," loving, but like Hellman, prone to temper. In the second portrait of *Pentimento*, Jenny's disapproval dissuades Hellman from her whimsical decision to go off with Willy, the mysterious and colorful businessman married to "ridiculous great-aunt" Lily of her mother's family. Hellman writes of these women throughout her memoirs, noting that in their house she "learned to laugh . . . and to knit and embroider and sew a straight seam and to cook," acknowledging too that what she learned from her aunts was far more important than how to make turtle soup: "They were fine women for a little girl to be around. . . . Later on, I knew that the things I learned from them would be good and valuable for me all my life."[12]

Obviously, Lillian Hellman revered these strong women and the insights about life that were their legacy to her; yet she was no more sentimental about her cherished aunts and Sophronia than she was about the South. Always, what makes Hellman's writing so intriguing is the questing, the refusal to accept anything at face value, the quality of a mind that insists not only on seeing but on "seeing again." An aged Hellman can see the pattern of her love for Sophronia in her tempestuous relationship years later with another treasured and strong-willed black servant, Helen; she can understand that "they were one person to you, these two black women you loved more than you ever loved any other women." She can recognize too that her image of Sophronia may well be false. She can at once cherish her beloved aunts and acknowledge their emotional shortcomings. Having created in *Toys in the Attic* two unmarried sisters whose emotionally incestuous attachment to their younger brother nearly destroys them all, twenty years later she writes of Jenny and Hannah that "without question, both my aunts were in love with their brother." This perception leads Hellman to sigh, "Ah, how much I had always wanted to be like my aunts and how much I feared being like them."[13]

In a 1979 interview, Hellman confided that she sometimes at night argued audibly with a part of her personality she called Nursie: "All my life I've divided myself into two and sometimes three parts," she explained.

12. Lillian Hellman, *Maybe* (Boston, 1980), 76, 83; Hellman, *An Unfinished Woman,* 17; Hellman, *Maybe,* 77.

13. Hellman, *Pentimento,* 3; Hellman, *An Unfinished Woman,* 230; Hellman, *Maybe,* 80, 82.

A third persona, Madam, reminds the squabbling pair that "there are two sides to everybody." Hellman knows that we have all known, at least since Freud, about the different, often antagonistic, components of our psyches. But her writing continues to speak to us because she demonstrates this perception in her constant probing of her own psyche. In *An Unfinished Woman* and repeatedly in interviews, Hellman acknowledged that from childhood she "lived within a question mark."[14] That interrogatory mode of existence, fostered by the unique ingredients of her early life in New Orleans—being an only child in a house full of adults; Jewish in a Protestant culture; homely in a society in which women were to be beautiful; and above all, bright and rebellious—is what distinguishes Lillian Hellman's work.

Hellman pretended to reject the past, yet her own past and the values and experiences of her youth figured throughout her work. As she aged, she turned more and more to her southern childhood in an attempt to come to terms with the complexities of her life and times. Her friend, fellow writer and New Orleanian Peter Feibleman, in his reminiscences of Hellman, wrote of the fillalloo bird, a wooden toy sold years ago in New Orleans that bore the legend, "I am the Fillalloo Bird. I fly backwards because I don't care where I'm going but I like to see where I've been." Feibleman notes that Hellman once admitted to her friend Dorothy Parker, "I *am* a Fillalloo Bird, I can't help it."[15] How like Hellman, to acknowledge her preoccupation with her past but also her ambivalence about it. Hellman's New Orleans is a psychic space that she approaches again and again with her proverbial question mark; tentatively, ambivalently, Hellman revisits the scene and the people of her youth. Compared to writers like Tennessee Williams and Walker Percy, she has contributed relatively little to the myth of a literary New Orleans, but a real New Orleans and its people reverberate throughout nearly every page of Lillian Hellman's work.

14. Marilyn Berger, "Profile: Lillian Hellman," in *Conversations with Lillian Hellman*, ed. Bryer, 263; Hellman, *An Unfinished Woman*, 119.

15. Feibleman, *Lilly*, 104.

Zora Neale Hurston
Courtesy Photographs and Prints Division, Schomburg
Centre for Research in Black Culture, New York Public
Library, Astor, Lenox and Tilden Foundations

The Neo-African Vatican:
Zora Neale Hurston's New Orleans

DAVID C. ESTES

In August, 1928, Zora Neale Hurston arrived in New Orleans, drawn by its reputation as home to some of the most powerful hoodoo doctors. She wanted to learn firsthand about hoodoo, the traditional African American belief in conjurors' ability to influence human lives and to control the course of events on behalf of their clients. According to Hurston's book of southern black folklore, *Mules and Men,* "New Orleans is now and has ever been the hoodoo capital of America." Previously, Hurston had collected charms from several conjurors in central Florida and in Mobile, Alabama. Her account of hoodoo beliefs and practices in New Orleans, however, is much more extensive because, as she says, "I had greater opportunity for study and greater leisure in New

Orleans than in Florida." She remained in the city for about six months, from the end of the sweltering summer through the mild winter months of 1929. During November and December of that year she returned, desiring "to make this conjure work very thorough and inclusive," as she wrote to Franz Boas, her anthropology professor at Columbia University.[1] These two trips were extremely productive. Hurston's accounts remain the only publications on hoodoo in the Crescent City written by a trained folklorist from an insider's point of view, and they are noteworthy not only as anthropological documents but also as literary texts.

Hurston wrote about conjure for distinctly different audiences—scholars and general readers, some interested in ethnographic fact and others in literature. The most academic piece, "Hoodoo in America," constituted an entire issue of the *Journal of American Folklore* in 1931. It is a one-hundred-page account based on her fieldwork in Florida, Alabama, and Louisiana, and it includes an extensive compilation of directions for making charms for various purposes. "Mother Catherine," originally included in Nancy Cunard's *Negro: An Anthology* (1934), is a character sketch of a popular New Orleans religious leader and her temple compound. Hurston's most widely read discussion of New Orleans, however, is the "Hoodoo" section that she inserted in *Mules and Men* (1935) to satisfy her publisher, who found her manuscript about Florida folklore to be of insufficient length for publication as a book.[2] All the material on hoodoo was extracted from her article previously published in the *Journal of American Folklore*. The resulting text is not simply an expedient reprinting, however. It conveys a deeper understanding of New Orleans' significant position on the national map of American culture because of the indigenous folkways of its African American residents.

As a group, these three pieces from early in Hurston's career depict the authentic New Orleans as radically different from the stereotypes commonly associated with its culture in the popular American imagination.

1. Zora Neale Hurston, *Mules and Men*, in *Folklore, Memoirs, and Other Writings*, ed. Cheryl A. Wall (New York, 1995), 176, hereinafter cited parenthetically by page number in the text; Zora Neale Hurston, "Hoodoo in America," *Journal of American Folklore*, XLIV (1931), 392; letter to Franz Boas, December 10, 1929, quoted in Robert E. Hemenway, *Zora Neale Hurston: A Literary Biography* (Urbana, 1977), 130. See 104–33 for details regarding Hurston's time in New Orleans and her relationship with Mrs. Rufus Osgood Mason, the patroness who sponsored her fieldwork.

2. Hemenway, *Zora Neale Hurston*, 163.

Stretching at least as far back as the 1803 Louisiana Purchase, New Orleans was identified with such sybaritic pleasures as food, music, dancing, gambling, and illicit sex. Its pestilential climate bred the undying spirit of *laissez le bon temps roulez*. It was a pagan city whose spirit of revelry, invoked annually at Mardi Gras, reigned throughout the year. Hurston repudiates the validity of these profane images by focusing on the sacred core of the city. More than "the hoodoo capital of America," New Orleans becomes a neo-African Vatican in which elements of Roman Catholic belief and ritual have been incorporated into a vibrant, traditional black religion. It is a holy metropolis, sacralized through folk rituals and various forms of traditional speech by which religious leaders regularly and confidently invoke the power of the spirit world into the lives of ordinary people.

In the recent enthusiasm for Hurston's work, scholars have given little attention to her depictions of urban African American life in New Orleans. Houston A. Baker, Jr., is an important exception. He argues that *Mules and Men* "is a *locus classicus* for black women's creativity" because it "amply defines the type of the conjure woman." Although attentive to issues of space and poetics in discussing the significance of the conjurer, Baker ignores New Orleans as an urban space in which Hurston found living hoodoo beliefs and practices. He speaks instead of the conjure woman herself "as a peculiar, imagistic, Afro-American space."[3]

Hurston's writings about New Orleans reveal an interest in the modern city that contrasts sharply with the rural settings of her fiction—and with the conclusions drawn by scholars who limit their reading to that part of her work. For example, Hazel Carby has suggested that "the creation of a discourse of 'the folk' as a *rural* people in Hurston's work in the 1920's and 1930's displaces the migration of black people to cities. Her representation of African American culture as primarily rural and oral is Hurston's particular response to the dramatic transformations within black culture."[4] As a generalization, this conclusion obscures the important fact that Hurston did not think of African American culture as *exclusively* rural and oral. The urban rituals enacted by New Orleans hoo-

3. Houston A. Baker, Jr., *Workings of the Spirit: The Poetics of Afro-American Women's Writing* (Chicago, 1991), 72, 79.

4. Hazel V. Carby, "The Politics of Fiction, Anthropology, and the Folk: Zora Neale Hurston," in *New Essays on "Their Eyes Were Watching God,"* ed. Michael Awkward (Cambridge, Mass., 1990), 76.

dooists of various types commanded her attention, too, and at an important period in her career. Carby correctly notes that Hurston's attention was not drawn to rapid social change. With an interest in folklore, Hurston understandably focused on continuities over time rather than on the "dramatic transformations" taking place in the lives of black migrants from southern farms. As an anthropologist looking at the black urban experience in New Orleans, she found a folk culture influenced by its African origins and the city's particular cultural history.

The New Orleans that Hurston rendered in these publications attracted her as an ethnographic site, a label that conveys much about the ideology that established her angle of vision. In the language of her academic discipline, she arrived in New Orleans as a "participant-observer" in and of its culture. Training in the social sciences invested her, in the minds of her contemporaries, with an empirical objectivity on which the reliability of her writings would rest. As Carby noted, Hurston thought of anthropology "as providing a professional point of view." This "professional gaze" radically separated Hurston from the traditional hoodoo community, despite their shared African American ethnicity. John Dorst contends that her fieldwork involved "the search for and participation in the authentic Other."[5]

The ultimate purpose of Hurston's venture, as for other anthropologists, was not immersion within the Other, despite intimate participation in it. The goal was rather a written record displaying intellectual control over the culture of the Other as the means of authenticating her professional status. Hurston's accounts of New Orleans hoodoo reveal, nevertheless, that her initiation experiences, essential to her participant-observer fieldwork methodology, had a much more profound personal meaning than her academic training suggested they would. The feelings she experienced as a hoodoo initiate caused her finally to regard as inadequate the ethnographic conventions in which she was trained. In her efforts to inscribe New Orleans, Hurston in the end drafted a less scientific text, in which at important points she describes the culture more creatively than objectively.

As a fieldworker, Hurston applied the principles of ethnography she had learned in the classroom of Franz Boas (1858–1942), the father of

5. *Ibid.*, 79; John Dorst, "Rereading *Mules and Men:* Toward the Death of the Ethnographer," *Cultural Anthropology,* II (1987), 309.

American anthropology. The students of this German Jewish immigrant at Columbia University included Ruth Benedict, Melville Herskovits, Margaret Mead, and Edward Sapir. Hurston worked with Boas while an undergraduate at Barnard in the late 1920s and again in 1935, following her fieldwork in New Orleans, during the semester she took doctoral coursework at Columbia. Robert Hemenway has commented that "she terminated those studies . . . partially because Columbia's preoccupation with Native Americans was impeding the research she had already begun. 'Pawnee is not likely to help me much in say, Alabama,' she said [in a letter]." Despite their differing research interests, Hurston applied Boas' basic tenets to African American folk culture. Most important among these are the concepts that "civilization is not something absolute, but that it is relative, and that our ideas and conceptions are true only so far as our civilization goes" and that "each and every civilization is the outcome of its geographical and historical surroundings."[6]

Boas therefore vigorously opposed evolutionary anthropologists and their "racial approach to the problem of human difference." Instead of race, he emphasized history. He based the scientific study of culture on "the history of the people, the influence of the regions through which they passed in migrations, and the people with whom they came into contact."[7]

Larry Neal is only partly correct in claiming that Hurston "approached her subject with the engaged sensibility of the artist . . . [and] would have been very uncomfortable as a scholar committed to 'pure research.'"[8] These two sensibilities, despite Neal's facile bifurcation of them, are complexly intertwined in Hurston's accounts of New Orleans. Boas' preface to *Mules and Men,* solicited by Hurston herself, is but one indication that she sought affirmation for applying accepted scholarly approaches to documenting black folk culture. He commended the book in part because "to the student of cultural history the material presented

6. Robert Hemenway, "Folklore Field Notes from Zora Neale Hurston," *Black Scholar,* VII (April, 1976), 39; Franz Boas, "The Principles of Ethnological Classification," in *The Shaping of American Anthropology, 1883–1911: A Franz Boas Reader,* ed. George W. Stocking, Jr. (New York, 1974), 66.

7. Melville Herskovits, *Franz Boas: The Science of Man in the Making* (New York, 1953), 26; Boas, "Principles," 66.

8. Larry Neal, "Zora Neale Hurston: A Profile," *Southern Exposure,* I (Winter, 1974), 166.

is valuable not only by giving the Negro's reaction to every day events, to his emotional life, his humor and passions, but it throws into relief also the peculiar amalgamation of African and European tradition which is so important for understanding historically the character of American Negro life, with its strong African background in the West Indies, the importance of which diminishes with increasing distance from the south" (3).[9] Boas applauded Hurston's perceptive treatment of black folkways within a context of historical displacement from Africa and interaction with European culture in the New World. Hurston's New Orleans thus cannot be entirely separated from the practice of anthropology in her day and Boas' commitment to the scholarly rejection of cultural evolutionists.

Hurston initially regarded New Orleans as an ethnographic site, having come to the city as a scientific researcher, not a tourist or freelance journalist. A thirst for knowledge, rather than the contentment of a comfortable ambience, motivated her explorations of the city. The demands of her research propelled her beyond the confines of the French Quarter, then a rather shabby area just becoming the fashionable residence for artists. She lived, at least for a time, on Belleville Court, a ferry ride across the Mississippi River from the French Quarter in the Algiers section, reputed to be the home of the legendary Seven Sisters of hoodoo. She also traveled to the eastern outskirts of the city, across the Industrial Canal into the Lower Ninth Ward, where many working-class blacks were then beginning to move into newly built residential neighborhoods.

Hurston therefore saw the city from the point of view of ordinary African American residents. While apprenticed to various hoodoo doctors, she listened to the woes of these citizens, who recounted their problems with unfaithful and lazy spouses, mothers-in-law, and court cases, their fears of being murdered, and the hoodoo curses put on them by enemies. Most of these people were poor black women, although some were upper class and white. Although other literary visitors between the wars came to work "in" the city, Hurston came to work "on" it—to document a slice of its life. Yet out of such scientific beginnings, she created in her writings a truly mythic city more powerful than the intoxicating scents of local color in the fiction of many authors.

9. Hurston received unsolicited acknowledgment of the merit of her research along these comparativist lines from Herskovits a few years later. In a discussion of the persistence of West African religious customs in the New World in the *Myth of the Negro Past* (1941), he favorably cites her documentation of hoodoo initiation rituals in New Orleans.

Hurston devotes two-thirds of "Hoodoo in America" to seven hoodoo practitioners from New Orleans. Four, including Marie Laveau, are grouped together as Catholic, two as Protestant, and one as having no religious affiliation. Hurston narrates charms that she observed being performed and describes several of her initiations into the work of conjurers. The discussion of each hoodooist concludes with a list of his or her spells for such particular purposes as influencing a court case, ensuring a lover's constancy, and causing physical pain or even death. After the section on New Orleans, Hurston discusses three other conjurers—two from Florida and one from Alabama. The article concludes with a brief section called "Use of the Dead in Conjure," eighteen conjure tales (five from New Orleans, the others from Florida, Georgia, and the Bahamas), and brief lists entitled "Paraphernalia of Hoodoo" and "Prescriptions of [unidentified] Root Doctors."

The opening of "Hoodoo in America" reveals the influence of Boas' central tenets of cultural anthropology on Hurston's fieldwork. She observes that hoodoo's "highest development [is] along the Gulf coast, particularly in the city of New Orleans and in the surrounding country." She attributes this phenomenon to history: "The Haytian emigrees [sic] at the time of the overthrow of French rule in Hayti by L'Overture . . . brought with them their hoodoo rituals, modified of course by contact with white civilization and the Catholic church, but predominantly African." Because of the differing system of slavery on the North American continent, tribal customs and African languages were generally lost there. Along the Gulf Coast, however, hoodoo found receptive host cultures, which influenced its development quite differently: "It took on characteristics of the prevailing religious practices of its immediate vicinity. In New Orleans in addition to herbs, reptiles, insects, it makes use of the altar, the candles, the incense, the holy water, and blessed oil of the Catholic church—that being the dominant religion of the city and state. But in Florida, no use is made of such paraphernalia. Herbs, reptiles, insects, and fragments of the human body are their stock in trade."[10] Her discussions of contemporary spiritualism in New Orleans and of obeah in the Bahamas, where Hurston conducted fieldwork on two trips in 1929 and 1930, provide a deeper understanding of the continuity and variation in the adaptation of African culture to varying New World settings.

10. Hurston, "Hoodoo in America," 318.

Following Boas, Hurston calls attention to the evolution of African culture in different geographic settings. Thus she links African American life in New Orleans historically to other precise locations, as if she were drawing a map. She does not portray the city as a culturally isolated locale. Instead, she traces the spatial and historic movement of hoodoo from Africa to the Caribbean into the United States through the port of New Orleans and then on into the Deep South. "Hoodoo in America" describes New Orleans as but one location along a global route of cultural transmission. Nevertheless, Hurston's map of the diaspora makes New Orleans the historic port of entry of African cultures to the American continent, as mediated through the Caribbean.

In the "Hoodoo" section of *Mules and Men,* Hurston reexamines the geographical and historical New Orleans by means of a new introduction and conclusion to a substantially shortened version of her "Hoodoo in America" article. The remaining narrative material about conjurors she reorganized into seven chapters. Among the omissions are the opening passages on how the slave economy linked New Orleans to the Caribbean and, from there, back to Africa. The second published version has Hurston entering New Orleans by car from central Florida, where she conversed about hoodoo with two women in Sanford and studied with another specializing in man-and-woman cases.

This new narrative bridges the geographic distance between Florida and New Orleans and also places ethnographic sites in the temporal sequence that Hurston visited them. She uses the metaphor of geography to call attention to the cultural relationships between New Orleans and black life in the rest of the United States. In her literary imagination, no longer is the city another Caribbean port; one reaches it by land from another southern state rather than by sea from the islands. In this way Hurston suggests that New Orleans, rather than the Caribbean, is the essential location for understanding the origins of black culture in this country. The symbolism in the new opening sentences of "Hoodoo" advances this point: "Winter passed and caterpillars began to cross the road again. . . . So I slept a night, and the next morning I headed my toe nails toward Louisiana and New Orleans in particular" (176). Although she actually arrived in late summer and stayed through early winter, the text is set in the season of spring, which corresponds to the vitality of its African American culture.

The conclusion to the "Hoodoo" section in *Mules and Men* further emphasizes the primacy of New Orleans as the center of African American culture. In the new version, having entered the city on an ethnographic mission, Hurston does not leave it, as she does in the previous version, when she heads farther east to Alabama and Florida. In the book, closure comes not through moving on but rather through the metaphor of "sitting," which she sums up with the lesson of a folktale. The dialect story of Sis Cat, who learns to eat a rat, follows Hurston's account of studying with the significantly named Kitty Brown. The story closes with the narrator declaring, "I'm sitting here like Sis Cat, washing my face and usin' my manners" (228). The moral of the tale conveys the necessity of staying in one place and adopting its ways in order to survive. Having learned from Sis Cat (and Kitty Brown), Hurston conveys a deep understanding of New Orleans and its hoodoo rituals as cultural models. New Orleans becomes a geographic center: it is a shrine to which pilgrims make their spiritual journey, rather than merely a stop along the way.

The revised geography in the *Mules and Men* "Hoodoo" text suggests Hurston's growing admiration for the religious folk traditions she documented in New Orleans, which she regarded as the essential embodiment of the vitality and life-enhancing power of African American traditional culture as a whole. Thus, for this book she revised not only the content but also the style of the opening pages of her earlier article. Mythic poetry replaces the scholarly, historical prose in the section of the book entitled "Origin of Hoodoo." Instead of writing as an objective outsider, she adopts the voice of the folk group she studied, using that community's characteristic idioms: "The way we tell it, hoodoo started way back there before everything" (176). Gone is her former care for historical accuracy, and in its place is an account in the style of folk history, those narratives shared orally among a group by which people memorialize their past. Given the African American community's low level of formal education about its past, the story of origins, not surprisingly, tends toward myth rather than history. Hurston tells how God created the world in "six days of magic spells and mighty words." Moses is "the first man who ever learned God's power-compelling words" (177), and the Queen of Sheba, who "had gold-making words" (177), was the one "who made Solomon wise." She gave him her "talking ring," to which he listened and "wrote down the ring-talk in books." Hurston closes with "that's what the old ones said in ancient times and we talk it again" (178).

A hoodoo altar. Note the pictures and effigies of the crucified Jesus and of saints, along with a bottle of rum, a boiled egg, and salt.
Courtesy New Orleans Historic Voodoo Museum

But in this section, Hurston does not scientifically document folk history. Metaphorically presenting her written text as talk, Hurston gives herself membership within the folk community and furthermore claims for her account of hoodoo, if not for *Mules and Men* as a whole, the same authenticity that a traditional performance possesses. This folk history links New Orleans to a mythic rather than historical Africa. The city becomes, then, an alternative site of America's national inception, a shrine counterpoised to Jamestown and Plymouth Rock. In this text, Hurston creates what Marjorie Pryse has called "a bridge between the *primitive* authority of folklife and the literary power of written texts."[11] The Crescent City becomes a New World center of the ancient mysteries of creative, spiritual power. Thus it is the urban mother of all African American culture, a sacred place where myth becomes a potent force in history.

The vivid narratives of Hurston's initiations by conjurers, repeated al-

11. Marjorie Pryse, "Zora Neale Hurston, Alice Walker, and the 'Ancient Power' of Black Women," in *Conjuring: Black Women, Fiction, and Literary Tradition,* ed. Marjorie Pryse and Hortense J. Spillers (Bloomington, 1985), 11.

most word for word in the two versions, have elicited a good deal of critical attention. But also deserving close attention are the descriptions of hoodoo altars documented in almost the same form in both the journal article and *Mules and Men*. These details have a richer metaphoric meaning in the latter text because of the mythic framework the revised introduction creates. In Hurston's descriptions of the construction and use of various altars, readers can note the folkloric principle of variation within continuity. The altar provides a focal point in group ceremonies, private meditation, and the making of charms. Its decorations include the doctor's symbolic source of power—a snakeskin in one instance and a large piece of brain coral in another. Ethnographically, Hurston's descriptions illustrate a Boasian concept: the dominance of Roman Catholicism in New Orleans influenced hoodoo there, in contrast to what has occurred in the rural, Protestant South.

The altars function in part by giving the rituals a customary location within the homes of hoodooists, thus linking ordinary people to the power of the mythic figures in folk history. This idea is vividly conveyed in Hurston's account of the setting for her ordination by Luke Turner: "At high noon I was seated at the splendid altar. It was dressed in the center with a huge communion candle with my name upon it set in sand, five large iced cakes in different colors, a plate of honeyed St. Joseph's bread, a plate of serpent-shaped breads, spinach and egg cakes fried in olive oil, breaded Chinese okra fried in olive oil, roast veal and wine, two huge yellow bouquets, two red bouquets and two white bouquets and thirty-six yellow tapers and a bottle of holy water" (191). Standing in front of this elaborate altar, Turner called out, "Spirit, I want you to take her, she is worthy" (192). Folk rituals enacted within the sacred space marked by an altar are intended to transfer spiritual power from the mythic past directly to the present. "Hoodoo in America" suggests a quite different source of spiritual power, one more in keeping with Boasian anthropology. Hurston's introduction to the article implies the mediation of African spiritual power through the historical movement of slaves to the New World. Within a few years, however, Hurston had come to a radically new understanding of the significance of ritual. In *Mules and Men,* ritual replaces history as her way of accounting for the presence of spiritual power in hoodoo. As Luke Turner says Marie Laveau told him: "Go to your own house and build an altar. Power will come" (185).

The custom of building hoodoo altars within domestic spaces reveals the rich aesthetic sense of the religion's adherents in New Orleans. The altars are diverse, as Hurston's descriptions reveal. Each one reflects the unique spiritual power and personality of its maker. But the altars are not completely dissimilar; they are constructed within the bounds of an un-written tradition governing the selection and display of sacred objects. Improvisation is the principle that determines the composition of each altar. Governed by the same aesthetic sense as other forms of black art, for example, jazz, the altars of New Orleans hoodoo convey the elemen-tal African American spirit. Within Hurston's ethnographic accounts, these altars are documentable artifacts of hoodoo. But scientific empiri-cism is only part of what impels her to record their design and ritual uses. By describing them in her texts, Hurston hopes to cast a spell of her own against the elite white culture that censured hoodoo's followers. Playfully improvisatory yet never provisional in their potency, the altars are con-jure sites that de-center power in order to sacralize New Orleans as the entryway for the African gods into the North American continent. Hoo-doo altars are a means of contesting the exclusive association of power with white commercial, judicial, and religious edifices and re-situating it within the homes of African Americans. Although protected from public view, the hoodoo altars in private, domestic spaces dominate the urban landscape of Hurston's New Orleans. Her translation of this ethno-graphic artifact into literary symbol suggests a cultural critique that goes far beyond what Boas had in mind when he called for "a consideration of the achievements of the Negro . . . and particularly of the culture that he has developed in his own natural surrounding."[12]

Hoodoo deconstructs not only white power but also male dominance. Hurston's New Orleans is a place for empowerment of and through women, even though her conjurors are not all women; of the seven from New Orleans mentioned in "Hoodoo in America," only two are women. Yet in "Hoodoo," Hurston revised the order so that the Florida root-worker Eulalia comes first, and Kitty Brown, last. Taking chronological as well as spiritual precedence over them all is Marie Laveau. Hurston is not careful in either of her versions to distinguish between historical fact and legend in the biographical details she presents. Most important, she conflates the two Maries, mother and daughter, into a single woman. The mother died on June 16, 1881, at the age of ninety-eight. Her daugh-

---

12. Quoted in Herskovits, *Franz Boas,* 111.

ter Marie Heloise (also called Euchariste) was born on February 2, 1827, the date given by Hurston. She also died in 1881, on an unknown date but after her mother. The mother's passing was prominently noted in the press. Interestingly, several writers eulogized her as a devout Catholic who had repented of her hoodooism. There is reason, however, to believe that these accounts owe much to the efforts of Marie Philomise Legendre, who cared for her mother in the house on St. Anne Street. Unlike the older Marie Heloise, Marie Philomise had never followed her mother into hoodoo work and sought to defend the family's reputation against its legendary association with the occult.[13]

Whereas the legends about Marie Laveau in "Hoodoo in America" come from the pen of the objective narrator, in the revised text Luke Turner recounts this folk history in his own voice to Hurston while they are seated "before the soft coal fire in his grate" (183). Hurston's decision to attribute these narratives to Turner, who says he received his hoodoo power directly from Laveau, suggests that spiritual women are models for all, both women and men, who wish to gain access to the power their cultural heritage offers. Turner ranks her among the most powerful con-jurers: "Moses had seen the Burning Bush. Solomon by magic knowed all wisdom. And Marie Laveau was a woman in New Orleans" (183). Her life in legend is intertwined with the history and geography of the city. Born of a white father and a quadroon mother, she was a child of the co-lonial custom of unofficial crossracial marriages. She annually celebrated the Feast of St. John, a Catholic holiday, to honor her hoodoo spirits. These rituals took place, Turner informs Hurston, at Bayou St. John, a landmark that connects the old city with Lake Pontchartrain. She appro-priated not only a spot on this bayou for her rituals but also her residence on St. Anne Street, where according to one legend she worked undis-turbed at her altar while the police tried unsuccessfully to enter and take her to jail. When Turner initiates Hurston a few pages after telling her these legends, the composite Marie Laveau of legend becomes her spiri-tual ancestress as well, thus advancing the author's claims for the authen-ticity of the New Orleans described in her texts.

13. The spelling of Marie's surname varies in the historical sources; contemporary writers most commonly use "Laveau." For the most complete and authoritative discus-sion of her biography, see Ina Johanna Fandrich, "The Mysterious Voodoo Queen Marie Laveaux: A Study of Power and Female Leadership in Nineteenth-Century New Orleans" (Ph.D. dissertation, Temple University, 1994), 240–73.

Mother Catherine Seal's statue at her gravesite, from *Gumbo Ya-Ya,* ed. Lyle Saxon (New York: Houghton-Mifflin, 1945)

This New Orleans is essentially female as well as essentially black. There is no greater contrast to this vision of the city than that by another near-contemporary transient resident there from the small-town South. In the well-known sketch published in 1925 in the *Double Dealer,* William Faulkner personifies New Orleans as "a courtesan, not old and yet no longer young, who shuns the sunlight. . . . She reclines gracefully upon a dull brocaded chaise-longue, there is the scent of incense about her, and her draperies are arranged in formal folds. . . . And those whom she receives are few in number, and they come to her through an eternal twilight. She does not talk much herself, yet she seems to dominate the conversation, which is low-toned but never dull, artificial but not brilliant. And those who are not of the elect must stand forever without her portals."[14] Hurston's personification of New Orleans is not Faulkner's high-class, effete whore. Rather, a vibrant, holy priestess presides over her city's rich African American culture.

Hurston's sketch "Mother Catherine" provides a striking contrast to Faulkner's courtesan. Mother Seal (*ca.* 1874–1930), with whom Hurston studied for two weeks, was affiliated with the Spiritual church, a denomination introduced to New Orleans in the early 1920s by a woman from Chicago.[15] In "Hoodoo in America" Hurston reported that "there are many advantages to a hoodoo doctor in embracing spiritualism. Hoodooism is in disrepute, and certain of its practices forbidden by law. A spiritualistic name protects the congregation, and is a useful devise of protective coloration."[16] Mother Seal's Temple of the Innocent Blood provided Hurston an opportunity to document the complex mingling of

14. Quoted in William Faulkner, *New Orleans Sketches,* ed. Carvel Collins (New Brunswick, N.J., 1958), 49.

15. Edward B. McDonald, "Catherine Seal," *Notable Black American Women,* II, ed. Jessie Carney Smith (New York, 1996), 581–86. Jason Berry illustrates his discussion of Mother Catherine with historic photographs in *The Spirit of Black Hawk: A Mystery of Africans and Indians* (Jackson, Miss., 1995), especially 74–75. Claude F. Jacobs and Andrew J. Kaslow provide an overview of this denomination in *The Spiritual Churches of New Orleans: Origins, Beliefs, and Rituals of an African-American Religion* (Knoxville, 1991). For further information on women in the Spiritual church, see David C. Estes, " 'Hoodoo? God do!': African American Women and Contested Spirituality in the Spiritual Churches of New Orleans," *Spellbound: Women and Witchcraft in America,* ed. Elizabeth Reis (New York, 1998).

16. Hurston, "Hoodoo in America," 319.

hoodoo beliefs and rituals with Roman Catholic and African American Protestant religious practices.

Mother Catherine's fenced compound of several buildings, popularly called the Manger, was a well-known attraction in the city's Lower Ninth Ward during the late 1920s. Its furnishings are, in Hurston's description, as exotic as those in the dwelling of Faulkner's courtesan: "a place of barbaric splendor, of banners, of embroideries, of images bought and images created by Mother Catherine herself; of an altar glittering with polished brass and kerosene lamps. There are 356 lamps in this building."[17]

Mother Catherine herself is a ruler whose charisma attracts followers, just as it compelled Hurston to revere her: "She might have been the matriarchal ruler of some nomad tribe as she sat there with the blue band about her head like a coronet; a white robe and a gorgeous red cape falling away from her broad shoulders, and the box of shaker salt in her hand like a rod of office. I know this reads incongruous, but it did not look so. It seemed perfectly natural for me to go to my knees upon the gravel floor, and when she signalled to me to extend my right hand, palm up for the dab of blessed salt, I hurried to obey because she made me feel that way." Despite many similarities to Faulkner's courtesan, Mother Catherine's words are not "artificial" but are the very breath of the spirit. Hurston records a number of her statements delivered probably as part of the sermon during public worship services. The spiritual power of women is one of her themes: "It is right that woman should lead. A womb was what God made in the beginning, and out of that womb was born Time, and all that fills up space. So says the beautiful spirit." Her authority for such pronouncements comes from the immediacy of her divine call: "Mother Catherine was not converted by anyone. Like Christ, Mohammed, Buddha, the call just came. No one stands between her and God." As Hurston notes without a trace of mockery, "Mother Seal takes her stand as an equal with Christ."[18]

Mother Catherine's temple compound, dedicated to providing a home for destitute women and unmarried mothers, is a metaphoric unfolding of the female essence of New Orleans that Hurston uncovered through her hoodoo research. Personified as African American and as woman, the

17. Zora Neale Hurston, "Mother Catherine," *Folklore, Memoirs, and Other Writings,* ed. Cheryl A. Wall (New York, 1995), 854.

18. *Ibid.,* 855, 857, 859.

city is the locus of an empowering traditional culture. Hurston's New Orleans is certainly a recognizable, historical place, described in what she considers trustworthy ethnographic detail. Yet in literature it is an unusual Crescent City for its time because she viewed it exclusively from an African American perspective. Paradoxically, while immersed in the historically determined culture of the city, Hurston had her eyes opened to the universal. Hoodoo's traditional rituals ultimately eluded her Western, scientific understanding by initiating her into an African, spiritual way of looking at the world. Thus the New Orleans in her texts transcends its location on the map of America in which she has metaphorically centered it. For her, New Orleans is the holy, the eternal, and the female, and the wellspring of its identity is the perpetual ritual enactment by its African American citizens of their religious folk culture.

Tom Dent, poet, playwright, and civil rights activist
Photo by Ellis Lucia, courtesy Tom Dent

Shared Traditions and Common Concerns: The African American Literary Community in Twentieth-Century New Orleans

VIOLET HARRINGTON BRYAN

Through formal and informal institutions, African American writers in New Orleans have created a framework for their literary activity. The writing community shares concerns and appreciates the uniqueness of its cultural traditions—the distinctive nature of African American music, food, family ties, and spiritual beliefs—both in New Orleans and throughout the country. Other African American institutions in New Orleans, such as black colleges, churches, newspapers, and writing and theater organizations, have also encouraged the writing community's many ventures. The work of a selected group of twentieth-century writers shows how these shared traditions and common concerns have supported literary production in New Orleans' African American community.

The first anthology of poetry by African American writers published in the United States, *Les Cenelles* (1845), was the work of a group of *gens de couleur libres* (free people of color) led by Armand Lanusse.[1] Free people of color also collaborated on the publication of several Reconstruction-era newspapers—*La Tribune de la Nouvelle-Orleans*, *L'Union*, the *Daily Crusader*—all of which fought against continuing encroachments on the rights of people of color. In the 1930s, the black unit of the WPA Federal Writers' Project, which met at Dillard University under the direction of Lawrence D. Reddick and then Marcus Bruce Christian, produced "A History of Black Louisiana," a manuscript that remains unpublished. Some of the group's research on African American culture and history in Louisiana was incorporated into books published by Lyle Saxon, Robert Tallant, and Edward Dreyer through the Louisiana Federal Writers' Project. Many African American writers of the 1930s and 1940s were also published in the "Poets' Corner" of the *Louisiana Weekly*, an African American newspaper, while Marcus Christian was poetry editor.

In the 1960s, the Free Southern Theater, started by a racially integrated group of playwrights and actors, became increasingly an African American organization after moving in 1964 to New Orleans, where it developed and performed original plays, with Gilbert Moses, Tom Dent, and John O'Neal adding to the repertoire.

More recently, the Tremé section of New Orleans remains a cultural district and source of creativity for most African American writers in the city. The Jazz and Heritage Foundation, which has presented an annual jazz festival in New Orleans since 1970, also promotes the work of many African American writers. The Alliance for Community Theaters, Inc. (ACT I), founded in 1978, has presented annual theater festivals of works by African American writers in the Mississippi Gulf area since 1982.

The Dillard Project essentially began with the *Louisiana Weekly*'s "Poet's Corner." Lyle Saxon, who was director of the Louisiana Federal Writers'

1. Armand Lanusse, ed., *Les Cenelles: Choix de poésies indigenes* (New Orleans, 1845). Published also as *Creole Voices: Poems in French by Free Men of Color* (Washington, D.C., 1945). Republished also as *Les Cenelles: A Collection of Poems by Creole Writers of the Early Nineteenth Century* (Boston, 1979).

Project, had learned about Marcus Christian's literary interests through reading his work in the *Weekly* and asked Christian to join the Dillard Project in 1936. In June, 1937, several contributors to the "Poet's Corner" published their poetry in a mimeographed volume, *From the Deep South.* The collection included poems by Marcus Christian, Octave Lilly (who published a book of poetry, *Cathedral in the Ghetto,* in 1973), Oscar Bouise, Ephraim D. Tyler, Inez Foster Jones, Edward Dejoie Burbridge, Clarence A. Laws, Thelma Seraile Mills, Lorraine Frilot, Peter Wellington Clark, Eugene B. Willman, Elton Williams, Homer Clyde McEwen, William Henry Huff, and L. Gully Carter.[2]

This collection and the "Poet's Corner" exemplify the kind of collaborative effort that characterizes much of the writing of African Americans in New Orleans. Most of these writers, lacking a general reading audience, did not get to be known outside their circle; only a few were published, either privately or in such journals and newspapers as *Crisis, Opportunity, Phylon,* the New York *Herald-Tribune,* and the Pittsburgh *Courier.* Several of them wrote prolifically, however. The Marcus Christian Collection at the University of New Orleans, for example, has 1,175 of Christian's poems, three of his plays (incomplete), his fiction, and voluminous notes and diaries. Christian's publications were printed privately and usually for special occasions. He wrote and published the long poems *In Memoriam—Franklin Delano Roosevelt* (1945) and *Common Peoples' Manifesto of World War II* (1948); the historical volume *Negro Soldiers in the Battle of New Orleans* (1955); a book of poetry, *High Ground* (1958), which he edited; the Whitmanesque poem *I Am New Orleans* (1968); and a historical work, *Negro Ironworkers of Louisiana, 1718–1900* (1972).

At Dillard, notable African American scholars and artists in the black WPA unit included Horace Bond, James LaFourche, Clarence Laws, Eugene Willman, and Homer McEwen. As director of the project, Marcus Christian was also acquainted with the works of other black leaders, among them Sterling Brown, who was director of the Washington, D.C., Federal Writers' Project at Howard University, and Margaret Walker, who attempted to join the New Orleans WPA but later went to Chicago,

2. Octave Lilly, *Cathedral in the Ghetto* (New York, 1970). For more information on the other poets and on *From the Deep South,* see Literary and Historical Manuscripts, Marcus Christian Collection, in Archives and Special Collections, University of New Orleans. Hereafter, the Marcus Christian Collection will be referred to as MCC.

where she worked with Richard Wright, director of Chicago's Federal Writers' Project for blacks. Randolph Edmonds, an important playwright in New Orleans, was sometimes associated with the group, as was Frank Yerby, who taught at Dillard for a few years during this time.[3]

Christian had the assistance of LaFourche, Bond, Reddick, and the other Dillard associates for his prodigious research on black Louisiana history. At the same time, he was writing poetry, stories, plays, and articles for the *Louisiana Weekly*. Christian and the other members of the Dillard Project amassed voluminous historical information that they planned to publish under the title "A Black History of Louisiana." At some point in their work, Christian recognized that the book would most likely never be published by Lyle Saxon and his associates. The history was still incomplete when the WPA ended the Writers' Project in 1942, but Christian was successful in getting a Rosenwald Fund fellowship to continue the work in 1944. The typescript and a microfilm copy are in the Marcus Christian Collection at the University of New Orleans.

In "History of Black Louisiana," the Dillard group intended primarily to clarify and revise misunderstandings of the role of blacks in Louisiana (and, by extension, in America). The writers pointed out that Africans came to America with valuable skills; they were iron-makers, blacksmiths, gold artificers, and wood carvers. They also brought strong religious beliefs and practices and were skilled in warfare. From their interviews with many former slaves, the researchers recounted slave life in New Orleans. (John Blassingame consulted Christian while writing his book *Black New Orleans* in 1973.) Christian and the other Dillard researchers also uncovered much information about hoodoo, practiced by many New Orleanians (white and black), and about the slave insurrections in Louisiana. They also wrote about the major contributions of African Americans to New Orleans culture as inventors, musicians, and soldiers. Special attention was given to the black social aid and pleasure

---

3. Unfortunately, Christian always believed that Yerby borrowed ideas for the plot and characters of his novel *The Foxes of Harrow* from a plantation novel Christian was writing. Christian wrote about the situation in his diary entry of September 1, 1948. He realized that he had typed his manuscript about the character Stephen Harrow with a typewriter he had given away two years before Yerby's book came out in 1946. Christian remembered that Frank Yerby had been over to his house with friends and colleagues one evening and all had read the story Christian was working on. See "Diary, Notes, Business Card," Box 1, MCC.

clubs and to the Creole language and culture. The final chapter of the unbound version of the history recounts the civil rights struggles of the 1930s and 1940s. As Joann Redding has noted, "They [the Dillard writers] saw hope in the rise of interracial organizations, white liberalism, and the increasing public recognition of African-American achievements."[4]

It is apparent from their work that the writers of the black Federal Writers' Project were integrationists. Christian's book of poetry, *High Ground* (printed in New Orleans in 1958), was written in commemoration of the U.S. Supreme Court's *Brown* v. *Board of Education* decision of May 17, 1954, to integrate the public schools. One of Christian's more famous poems, "Segregation Blues," concludes the volume. All too conscious of African American soldiers' participation in World War II (the "War for Democracy") and America's regession in terms of civil rights for African Americans, Christian's persona laments:

Got corns and bunions,
But I'm gonnah wear out all my shoes,
Oh, I can't go here,
I live there I'm dead,
And Uncle Sam himself
Can't tell me where to lay my head—
Like Mister Hitler's Jews,
I got thuh Segregation Blues—
Got thuh Housing Project, Street-car,
Jim-Crow, Segregation Blues.[5]

Another major collaborative effort among the city's African American writers was the Free Southern Theater, founded by John O'Neal, Doris Derby, and Gilbert Moses to answer the need for a theater in the South during the civil rights movement. The theater originally had its base in Jackson, Mississippi. Its mission was to foster community thinking about the tumultuous change being wrought by the movement and to expand the limited educational opportunities for southern blacks. In its early years, the theater produced plays by contemporary black and white writ-

4. John W. Blassingame, *Black New Orleans, 1860–1880* (Chicago, 1973); Joann Redding, "The Dillard Project: The Black Unit of the Louisiana Writers' Project," *Louisiana History*, XXXII (Winter, 1991), 58.

5. Literary and Historical Manuscripts, MCC.

"Hold on . . . we're coming!" from a 1969 poster advertising the Free Southern Theater
Courtesy Free Southern Theater Collection, Amistad Research Center at Tulane University

ers. The repertoire included *Purlie Victorious* by Ossie Davis, *Happy Ending* by Douglas Turner Ward, Martin Duberman's *In White America,* and Samuel Beckett's *Waiting for Godot.* When the theater moved to New Orleans in 1964 and opened offices in the Desire Housing Project, it continued with its original repertoire at first, although early shows also included Berthold Brecht's *The Rifles of Senora Carrar.* But the call to produce more plays by African American writers became imperative.[6] Tom Dent, who had just returned from New York and the Umbra literary workshop, became chairman of the board of directors.[7]

The Free Southern Theater found appreciative audiences but ignited a controversy in New Orleans' city government when it presented a poetry show, "The Ghetto of Desire," which was filmed by CBS for its television

6. Thomas C. Dent, Richard Schechner, and Gilbert Moses, eds., *The Free Southern Theater by the Free Southern Theater* (Indianapolis, 1969).

7. The Umbra poets included David Henderson, Calvin Hernton, Ishmael Reed, Bob Kaufman, Lorenzo Thomas, and Ted Joans.

program *Look Up and Live.* The show dramatically brought to light the poverty and political powerlessness of Desire Project residents. Gil Moses' play *Roots* also helped make people more aware of racial issues.[8]

As administrative problems mounted and members of the theater started to leave, the theater broadened its focus to include other types of writing. In December 1968, the first of a series of publications from the Free Southern Theater's writing and acting workshop, BLKART-SOUTH, was published privately. Tom Dent and Val Ferdinand (Kalamu ya Salaam) were coeditors of BLKARTSOUTH's journal, *Echoes from the Gumbo,* later retitled *Nkombo.* An objective of the workshop was to create new dramatic material for the Free Southern Theater. In the first issue, Dent noted that "this workshop was created as part of our program because we know that for a black theater to have viability in our communities we must have a working tie to those communities—something more than mere performances of plays every now and then (no matter how relevant the material). The community must have a stake in the life of the theater. This is the real meaning of community theater."[9] BLK-ARTSOUTH became an arena for the writing and critiquing of poetry much more than theater, poetry that reflected the ideals of the Black Aesthetic Movement of the 1960s. Several members of the group, among them Quo Vadis Gex-Breaux, Nayo (Barbara Watkins), Raymond Washington, and Ronald Fernandez, also published volumes of poetry. The final issue of *Nkombo,* published in July, 1974, paid tribute to black jazz and blues and celebrated the poetry and music of earlier generations. In addition to contributions by BLKARTSOUTH members, it included poems and prose by Marcus Christian and Octave Lilly, Richard Haley, and the young Alice Walker.[10]

Tom Dent's play *Ritual Murder,* which grew out of the Free Southern Theater's demand for viable black theater, was first performed under the direction of Chakula cha Jua at the Ethiopian Theater in New Orleans in

8. Dent *et al.,* eds., *Free Southern Theater,* 133, 123–35.

9. Thomas C. Dent, editorial, *Echoes from the Gumbo,* December, 1968, p. 3.

10. Richard Haley, a poet and civil rights activist whom James Baldwin discussed in his essay "They Can't Turn Back," continued to write poetry until his death in 1989. He was the husband of Oretha Castle Haley, well-known political activist during the civil rights movement. Alice Walker was at that time in the process of publishing several of her early works: *Once, The Third Life of Grange Copeland,* "Revolutionary Petunias" and Other Poems and In Love and Trouble.

1976.[11] Dent's play, like his poetry in *Magnolia Street* and *Blue Lights and River Songs,* deals with ordinary people, mostly black New Orleanians seeking self-expression in and through their environment.[12] In *Ritual Murder,* Dent portrays the cultural experience of Joe Brown, Jr., a young black man from the Desire Project. The narrator asks all those who know Joe Brown well why the young man killed his best friend at a bar on Saturday night. Nobody knows, but all have their theories. When the dead victim, James Roberts, is questioned, he reveals that Joe's anger mounted irrationally when James told him, "I don't understand all this blues over what happens everyday. He said he wanted to believe there is hope. I told him there is no hope. You a black mother-fucker and you may as well learn to make the best of it." But James doesn't blame Joe for killing him: "It happens all the time. I accept it. Joe is still my friend. Friends kill each other all the time . . . unless you have an enemy you can both kill." Dent's play resonates in the present as much as it did in the 1970s, perhaps even more so. Today, New Orleans has one of the highest homicide rates among American cities.

Tom Dent has continued to write and promote the writing of other young black authors. The Congo Square Writers' Workshop succeeded BLKARTSOUTH. Directed by Dent, the group published the journal *Bamboula* in 1976 and several issues of its newspaper, the *Black River Journal.* Its purpose was similar to that of *Nkombo:* "to give the 'Southern' writer a vehicle for publication and . . . to document emphatically the 'Southern Experience,' particularly the New Orleans experience."[13]

Dent's latest book, *Southern Journey: A Return to the Civil Rights Movement* (1997), explores new territory. For that project, Dent traveled through many small towns all over the South and conducted oral interviews with people who had been actively involved in the civil rights movement.[14] Kim Lacy Rogers has noted that "Tom Dent's aesthetic

11. Thomas C. Dent's *Ritual Murder* was first published in *Callaloo,* I (February, 1978), 67–81. It is reprinted in John Oliver Killens and Jerry W. Ward, Jr., eds., *Black Southern Voices: An Anthology of Fiction, Poetry, Drama, Nonfiction, and Critical Essays* (New York, 1992), 315–25. Further quotations in this paragraph are from p. 322 of this edition.

12. Tom Dent, *Magnolia Street* (New Orleans, 1976); Dent, *Blue Lights and River Songs* (Detroit, 1982).

13. Congo Square Writers' Workshop, *Bamboula* (July, 1976), 3.

14. Thomas C. Dent, *Southern Journey: A Return to the Civil Rights Movement* (New York, 1997).

struggle replicated the journeys of his colleagues in New Orleans' black protest generation. They were people who consciously maintained a connection with the black heritage that all were trained, by education and by opportunities for mobility, to escape. Through the movement, all had become conscious of their roots in black folk culture, and in the efforts of their immediate predecessors—the ambitious parents, teachers, and preachers who counseled hard work and racial uplift, striving and ceaseless struggle."[15]

Kalamu ya Salaam, a former editor of *Black Collegian* and executive director of the New Orleans Jazz and Heritage Foundation, continues to write, edit, and produce publications. In his book *What Is Life? Reclaiming the Black Blues Self* (1994), Salaam reflects on the civil rights and black power struggles, the personal and societal costs and rewards. He describes the "blues aesthetic" as including a sense of humor or exaggerated commentary on reality, brutal honesty, acceptance of the contradictory nature of life, faith in the ultimate triumph of justice, and celebration of the sensual and the erotic.[16] He sees the African American blues aesthetic as the best hope for coping with life.

Community theater is thriving in New Orleans and is supported through several important venues. ACT I, which in 1996 held its fourteenth annual New Orleans Black Theater festival, is a major force in promoting the city's various community theaters. For many years, Chakula cha Jua has helped lead this organization and its various member companies, among them the Ethiopian Theater, the Curtain Call Theater Company, Junebug Productions, the Chakula cha Jua Theater Company, and the ACT I Players. Junebug Productions originated with the folktales and anecdotes of John O'Neal's storyteller character, Junebug Jabbo Jones, in a one-man show. The Free Southern Theater, the Daishiki Theater led by Ted Gilliam, the groundbreaking Broadway plays *El Hajj Malik* by Norbert Davidson, and *One Mo' Time* by Vernel Bagneris, along with many other theater groups and dramatic productions, have been created because of the rich history of black theater in New

---

15. Kim Lacy Rogers, *Righteous Lives: Narratives of the New Orleans Civil Rights Movement* (New York, 1993), 188–89.

16. Kalamu ya Salaam, *What Is Life? Reclaiming the Black Blues Self* (Chicago, 1994), 13–14. Kalamu ya Salaam has published several books of poetry and plays, including the plays *BLK Love Song #1, Somewhere in the World (Long Live Assata),* and *The Quest.*

Kalamu ya Salaam, playwright and coeditor of *Nkombo*,
the publishing venture of BLKARTSOUTH
Courtesy Kalamu ya Salaam

Orleans and its cooperation with churches, schools, and community groups.

The collaborative impulse has waned somewhat among New Orleans writers, but it is still present. In the works of many women writers, we hear personal voices concerned with recovering the lost truths of New Orleans culture, particularly the attitudes, experiences, and consciousness of Afro-Louisianians, especially those of women.

Sybil Kein is a New Orleans-born poet, dramatist, musician, and scholar whose major interest is in preserving and re-creating the history, folklore, and language of the Louisiana Creole culture. In her first book of poetry, *Gombo People* (1981), written in both Louisiana Creole and English, Kein preserves for posterity the language and the ceremonies so important in the lives of the Creoles of New Orleans.[17] Stories of the past abound in these poems. For example, "Toucoutou" is based on a court case of the early 1900s in which a woman found to have some black ancestry brought suit to retain her status as white but lost the court decision. In Kein's poem, the focus is on the woman herself—her anger, shame, shock, and the evidence of French, Indian, and African ancestry behind her "taut blue veins" and "faint skin." Toucoutou's self-image vanishes before this loss of the "infinite untouchable / privilege of being / white," which is society's standard of beauty and acceptance. Kein describes Toucoutou as having the accepted white face—"rose-bud mouth, small French nose, Indian-brown hair curved to frame the portrait"—but showing behind the white appearance is the "ghost-grey" of slave ancestors, and when the court declares her black, her apparently white image vanishes, as her face is consumed by anger and self-hatred.

Some of Kein's poems are more humorous and lighthearted. A wry sense of humor comes through in such poems as "Cofaire?" ("How Come?"), from her second book, *Delta Dancer*.[18] Here Kein alludes to the popular misconception that Cajuns are white, whereas Creoles of color are black, even if they are *cousines*. She simulates the Creole dialect:

My cousine Tee-Ta, she say she Cajun;
et me, I'm Creole, name Tee-Teen.
She still live up on de Bayou, you know,
but me, I move to New Orleen.

The cousins have the same last name, Boudreaux; they cook the same food and like to dance and sing; but when the Cajun cousin comes to New Orleans, she says she's white and doesn't speak to her Creole cousin:

Well, *dit pas rien*, she do what she please,
and me, I just laugh all de time.
"Cajun" and "creole," we cousine, that's for true,
cause her "French" folks is "French"—same as mine!

The speaker is interested in the French ancestry that connects them; the cousins are united by the French connection, even if not by the African.

17. Sybil Kein, *Gombo People: Poésie Creole de la Nouvelle Orléans* (New Orleans, 1981).

18. Sybil Kein, *Delta Dancer: New and Selected Poems* (Detroit, 1984).

Sybil Kein, poet, playwright, and folklore scholar
Photo by Lisa C. Martin

In Kein's latest book, *The American South,* she continues to develop the themes of Creole life in Louisiana but adds more memories of the horrors and violence of slavery and the convoluted history of race across the South.[19] Still, in some of her best poems, one finds dramatic characters and scenes from New Orleans and memories of family, as in the poem "Legacy," in which the speaker remembers her father and his personal heroism:

If he had dreams of personal glory,
fortune, we never knew them.
We only knew he could grow a tree
from seeds, take an animal from death's

19. Sybil Kein, *The American South* (East Lansing, Mich., 1996).

Brenda Marie Osbey, a poet whose work reflects the Tremé
cultural district, which includes the old Congo Square
Photo by Chandra McCormick, courtesy Brenda Marie Osbey

mouth with a secret herb, cure the stinging wounds of
    children with
ancient remedies, give them joy
on sleepless cold nights with stories
about "Patcherah," or a magic trick, or
dancing fingershadows of swans on the
walls.

Like Kein, Brenda Marie Osbey re-creates the experiences, attitudes,
ways of seeing, and consciousness of the people she knows best—Afro-
Louisiana women. Her poetic community in her first three collections of

poetry, *Ceremony for Minneconjoux* (1983), *In These Houses* (1988), and *Desperate Circumstance, Dangerous Woman* (1991), is based largely on the Tremé area of New Orleans and the surrounding parishes and bayous of Louisiana.[20] But her landscape is more internal than physical. It is a religious and cultural terrain that readers cross as they imagine the characters and places that Osbey creates in her poems. In "Geography," from *In These Houses,* the speaker describes her mission as poet/historian:

> the geography i am learning
> has me place myself
> at simultaneous points
> of celebration
> and all you see and hear in me
> is these women
> walking in the middle of the road
> with their hoodoo in their hands.
>
> .   .   .   .
>
> this place no one chooses
> is the land i tarry in.
> This ritual i go through
> is as old as its name
> and the prophet-women who dance it.
> *First you place one foot*
> *and then the other.*

The speaker has remembered the past and re-created it for others, one step at a time. She has built her familial, ancestral past in her poetry, and in reading these poems we may conjure our past and enrich our lives.

Osbey uses blues, call-response rhythms, ring games, and hoodoo

---

20. Brenda Marie Osbey, *Ceremony for Minneconjoux* (Callaloo Poetry Series, Lexington, Ky.; rpr. Charlottesville, Va., 1985); *In These Houses* (Middletown, Conn., 1988); *Desperate Circumstances, Dangerous Woman: A Narrative Poem* (Brownsville, Ore., 1991); and *All Saints: New and Selected Poems* (Baton Rouge, 1997). For an informative study of the history of the Tremé district, see the series by Brenda Marie Osbey, "Faubourg Tremé: Community in Transition," New Orleans *Tribune,* December, 1990, January, 1991, and August, 1991.

characters, traditions, and ceremonies in the development of her narrative poems. Her characters recur in subsequent poems and form their own poetic community. As Calvin C. Hernton remarks about Osbey's poetry, "In addition to influences from the American Indian and French and Spanish cultures, the styles of speech and the general aura of the women reflect a certain African mystique . . . carried over into the New World and blended with the indigenously developed folkness of southern black women."[21] Although her characters reflect the various cultures that have influenced their lives, they are primarily engaged in expressing their personal blues and finding grace or healing through the community. Throughout her poems, there is great respect for ancestors and the community and a haunting sense of their presence.

Quo Vadis Gex-Breaux, a contributor to BLKARTSOUTH publications and the author of *Dark Waters,* a collection of poetry published in the late 1960s, has had many poems published in local and national journals, including the *Xavier Review,* the *New Laurel Review,* the *Black River Journal, Word Up,* and the *African American Review.* She is also a contributor to *Life Notes: Personal Writings by Contemporary Black Women,* edited by Patricia Bell-Scott. Gex-Breaux's poetry carefully blends metaphor, language, and rhythm.

Along with Gex-Breaux's mature lyricism is a strong social consciousness that finds expression in such poems as "Night Raid," the title alluding to the murderous police raid on the Algiers-Fischer Housing Project in 1980, which left several of the project's inhabitants dead.

> There was one witness
> but the papers did not say so
> neither did the police
> perhaps he was too small to mention
> so small so small
> hardly there at all
> peering out behind the bathroom door
>
> . . . .
>
> He was easily taken care of
> tossed inside the next-door neighbor's living room

21. Calvin C. Hernton, "The Tradition," *Parnassus,* XIII (Spring, 1985), 518–50.

Quo Vadis Gex-Breaux, poet and social critic, who participated in the
BLKARTSOUTH movement
Photo by Lloyd Dennis, courtesy Quo Vadis Gex-Breaux

as some closing act of kindness
an end to a bloody sacrificial feast

What could he say in court
that would be believed?

No one would listen to the recurring nightmare
of a four-year-old
who could have fantasized
his mother's cries for mercy
her pleading for her life
before her bath became her blood

It really doesn't matter but
there was one witness.[22]

Mona Lisa Saloy, author of the chapbook *Between Laughter and Tears: Black Mona Lisa Poems,* creates songs of New Orleans culture and its people.[23] Family is very important to her, as are the distinctions made by black Creole society on the basis of color, hair, and facial features. Saloy says that "she writes to speak for those who don't, to learn their lessons, and to celebrate their spirits." She is steeped in New Orleans culture. As she points out, "When a kid—say me—did something bad, my mother would not say, 'The boogie man will get you!' Instead, she would holler: 'I'll get Marie LaVeau for you!' " Many such characters are found in her work. "My wish for my work is to accomplish painting how Black folks self-determine in New Orleans or Oakland imagination, how they resonate with days that are songs seldom heard or felt, telling it like we do, for the last time."[24]

In her poems, Saloy uses refrains, blues, vendors' cries and songs—all types of New Orleans music and sounds. Her women are Creoles of color known by the people of the streets; they are "huckabuck women," "buck-head red sisters"—for the most part, Creole women of the Seventh Ward, where Saloy grew up. She writes poems about family and community. In one poem, the persona describes her admiration for her sister, eight years her elder, with her "Tchoupitoulas smile" and "jet black braids" who moved west to Seattle to escape the Jim Crow South. In other poems, her mother, father, and ancestors all come to life, as does the community of which they are a part. Playing games as children with Coke bottle caps and mosquito hawks, listening to the recordings of John Coltrane, Nat King Cole (from whose song the poet got her name), Brooke Benton, Dinah Washington, Ella Fitzgerald, Miles Davis, and to Mardi Gras songs like "Ike-ko, Ike-ko,/ Ike-ko Ikko-ko ande/ Jock-a-mo-fino a-na-nay,/ Jock-a-mo-fina-nay," or songs about "khaki boys and navy pleated girls" walking to school, eating their bag lunch of peanut butter or cold chicken necks with plantains or banana fritters for dessert,

---

22. Patricia Bell-Scott, ed., *Life Notes: Personal Writings by Contemporary Black Women* (New York, 1994), 324.

23. Mona Lisa Saloy, *Between Laughter and Tears: Black Mona Lisa Poems* (New Orleans, 1995).

24. Biographical statements of Mona Lisa Saloy, Typescript, n.p.

Mona Lisa Saloy, whose poems reflect life in the Seventh Ward
in New Orleans
Photo by James Terry III

or about jambalaya and red-wine dinners, mirliton, parsley, onion to
taste, and listening to the pecan vendor at the French Market, watching
the numbers man with his Dream Book, Mona Lisa Saloy tells intimate
tales of her neighborhood, her heritage:

> No one yells
> cause we carry
> "how're ya doing's" and
> "s'il vous plaits" between
> "pas connais."
> We save our clothes,
> make groceries, wash and scrub the porch and
> the banquette with lye

after hucklebuck spills
or boiled crawfish leavings
to clean and erase evil spells.[25]

The African American writers of New Orleans have contributed greatly to the city's literary image. New Orleans culture, as portrayed in their writings, is steeped in Kalamu ya Salaam's "blues aesthetic." Along with that aesthetic goes a fascination and respect for the elders, the folk-lore, and the history of the African American New Orleans community.

Other African American writers of New Orleans who are making names for themselves and adding to the lineage of writers from this city include Louis Edwards, who has published two novels, *Ten Seconds* (1991) and *N: A Romantic Mystery* (1977). In 1987, Fatima Shaik, a New Orleans native who lives in New York, published three novellas about voices of New Orleans, which appeared as *The Mayor of New Orleans: Just Talking about Jazz* (1987). Malaika Favorite, artist and writer from Louisiana, displayed both talents and explored the inner world of the spirit in her book *Illuminated Manuscript: Poems and Prints* (1991). In a fictionalized version of the life of Marie Laveau, Jewell Parker Rhodes adds to the myths of the city in her popular book *Voodoo Dreams: A Novel of Marie Laveau* (1993). The strength of African American writing in New Orleans from its beginnings through the writings of the WPA, the civil rights movement, and today has been the strength of its resilient sense of community.

25. Saloy, *Between Laughter and Tears*, 5, 9, 23.

John Kennedy Toole

Another Kind of Confederacy: John Kennedy Toole

W. KENNETH HOLDITCH

In 1976, Walker Percy agreed to teach a novel-writing course at Loyola University in New Orleans. Once a week, he drove across the lake from his home in Covington several hours before class to make himself available for conferences with his twelve students. He arrived one afternoon to find waiting for him a woman in her seventies attired in a formal fashion evocative of an earlier age: a lace-trimmed dress, a pillbox hat with a small veil, and white gloves. Staring from her round, carefully powdered face were the intense eyes of the true believer. She addressed him as "Dr. Percy," ceremoniously thrust a parcel into his hands, and in a strongly projected voice reminiscent of old-time stage actresses, commanded him, "Read this!"[1]

When she introduced herself as Thelma Ducoing Toole, Percy recognized the name of the woman who had called and written a number of times to plead with him to read her dead son's novel. That afternoon, she proceeded to relate the tragic story of "my son, the genius John Kennedy Toole"—the rejection of his novel by a New York publisher, the resultant despair and subsequent suicide—in an emotional style suggestive of an incantation, the archetypal and timeless voice of maternal lamentation, no less sincere for being in this instance very theatrical. Since the death of her son, she told him, she had submitted the work to several publishers, all of whom had rejected it; then, having read about Percy's course at Loyola, she had determined to bring him the manuscript. "Dear Dr. Percy," she said, "you must help me!"

Percy, a generous and gentlemanly man who found it difficult to refuse any request for assistance, much less one delivered in person by an elderly grieving mother and accompanied by such a tragic story, had often found himself in the unhappy position of reading unsolicited manuscripts that arrived in the mail, talking to aspiring writers who phoned or even appeared uninvited and unannounced at his door, or submitting to interviews from critics and journalists. Reluctantly, he agreed to read Toole's novel and ushered the effusively grateful Mrs. Toole from his office with a promise to contact her soon.

When he had finished his class and returned home, he began to read the bulky, battered typescript and found himself after a few pages startled, enchanted, amazed. This was not the novel he had anticipated—an amateur effort that would have required his once again disappointing the grieving mother by informing her that it was unpublishable—but a stunningly innovative work, sui generis, which made him

---

1. Much of the material in this essay derives from my numerous interviews and conversations with Thelma Toole between 1980 and 1984 and from unpublished material that she shared with me. In addition, I have interviewed many people who knew John Kennedy Toole, including William D. Horan, Earl Larre, Betty Caldwell, and Thomas Bonner. The research done by Dalt Wonk for articles on Toole and the interview conducted by Jesse Core with Mrs. Toole were also valuable. Quotations from Toole's letters are used with the permission of the Manuscripts Department, Howard-Tilton Memorial Library, Tulane University.

"gape, grin, laugh out loud, shaking my head in wonderment," as he later wrote in his introduction to the work.[2] Not only was the novel as remarkable as Mrs. Toole had insisted, but he doubted that even she had conceived of the full measure of its power.

Percy had the manuscript retyped and submitted it to several commercial publishers, all of whom rejected it, even though it was accompanied by his endorsement. Finally, Louisiana State University Press agreed to publish it, primarily out of respect for Percy, and in 1980, the small first edition of *A Confederacy of Dunces* made its appearance and immediately was sold out. The critical response was almost universally positive, and within a year Toole's novel was awarded the Pulitzer Prize, eleven years after his death at his own hands. Subsequently, it has left millions of readers, American and foreign, gaping, grinning, laughing, shaking their heads in wonderment at its improbable but unforgettable "hero" and his bizarre actions and the verbal pyrotechnics of the narrative.

The life of the author who did not live to reap either the financial or psychological advantages of the tremendous success of his work was in many respects typical of life as it is lived in New Orleans. He was born late in the lives of his parents on December 17, 1937, son of a father of Irish descent and a mother whose ancestors included not only Irish laborers who immigrated to the United States in the nineteenth century but also early French settlers of south Louisiana. Both parents had grown up in the Faubourg Marigny, the city's oldest suburb, later immortalized by Tennessee Williams as the setting for *A Streetcar Named Desire*. By 1900, it had become the shabby genteel home for an ethnic amalgam, commented on by the playwright in his stage directions. The French Creoles had, for the most part, vacated the district, leaving it to a mixture of Italian, Irish, and black residents. Indeed, Mrs. Toole's family, the Ducoings, were one of the few Creole families still living in the Marigny, and Thelma Toole took great pride in her French heritage; when he was a child, she often took her son to St. Louis Cemetery Number One to see the grave of his Ducoing ancestor who had fought as a gunner in the Battle of New Orleans in 1815.

2. Walker Percy, Foreword to *A Confederacy of Dunces* (New York: Grove Press, Evergreen Edition, 1987), 8. Subsequent references to the novel will be to this edition and will be included in the text.

Following their marriage, Thelma and John Toole also left the Marigny to settle uptown, a move that represented for them a step up the social ladder in a city in which each district has its own identity and measure of prestige, and in that part of the city their son was born. From early childhood, Ken Toole, as his family called him, was exceptional, and his mother, whose persistent dream of a theatrical career for herself had been thwarted by a combination of circumstances, made certain that he received all the cultural advantages their budget could provide. She saw to it that all the books she considered classics were available to him, reading to him until he was able to read for himself. In his first years of schooling, Ken showed signs of superior intellect, skipping two grades and consistently ranking first or near the top in his classes.

The image Ken Toole projected to teachers and other adults during his childhood and teen years was that of the "perfect young gentleman," well dressed, well mannered, and attentive to his elders. His contemporaries found him to be, though never an extrovert, nevertheless friendly, humorous, and always studious. By the time he was in kindergarten, he was already being trained by his mother, a teacher of elocution and the "dramatic arts," as a performer. She organized a group of young students into the Junior Variety Performers, with her chubby, cheerful young son as a star. Under her direction, the group performed at hospitals, orphanages, and other institutions, their programs consisting of songs, dances, and recitations composed by Mrs. Toole. An avid and eclectic reader, Ken began to write seriously at least as early as his high school years, and when he was sixteen and a senior, he produced a short novel, *The Neon Bible,* for submission to a contest. The summer before, he had spent several days with a school friend in rural Mississippi, the setting for this first sustained work of fiction. At about the same time, he learned to drive, and one afternoon he took his mother in the family car to the western part of New Orleans to point out to her a new church topped with a large neon sign in the shape of a cross. When *The Neon Bible* did not win the contest, he submitted the work to a publisher; after its rejection there, he seems to have lost interest in it. Later, he would comment slightingly of the early novel to Robert Gottlieb, the editor at Simon and Schuster who first accepted, then rejected *A Confederacy of Dunces.*

After graduating from high school as the "Most Intelligent Student," Ken Toole was awarded a National Merit Scholarship and attended Tulane University, where he first studied engineering, at his father's insistence, then became an English major with a concentration on medieval and Renaissance courses. His grades were excellent in all subjects except science, and he became proficient in Spanish. College friends remember him as quiet and reserved but surprisingly capable of mimicking or even mocking his contemporaries and professors with a wryly understated and generally unmalicious wit. In his senior year, 1957, he was inducted into Phi Beta Kappa and awarded a Woodrow Wilson Fellowship for graduate study.

He chose Columbia University for his master's degree, and for the first time he lived away from home for an extended period. In New York he took whatever advantage of the city's cultural and entertainment benefits his limited resources would permit and continued to distinguish himself in his studies. As his knowledge increased, so did the sharply intellectual quality of his wit. Though friends from the New York days recall that he could sometimes be merciless in his attack, he remained, for all of them, a southern gentleman, kind, considerate, and dependable. In one year he completed the requirements for the M.A. in English, writing a thesis on John Lyly, the sixteenth-century English author whose *Euphues,* a prose narrative written in extremely ornate and verbose language that came to be known as "euphuism," was later to manifest itself in *A Confederacy of Dunces.*

After graduation, Ken Toole remained in New York to teach freshman and sophomore courses at Hunter College and registered as a part-time Ph.D. candidate at Columbia. During this period he began work on the novel that would become *A Confederacy of Dunces;* in early drafts, the malcontented protagonist bore the name Humphrey Trueblood. At the end of the academic year, Toole accepted a teaching position for fall, 1959, at Southwestern Louisiana State University in Lafayette, where each semester he taught four freshman composition classes, an experience he later described in a letter to Robert Gottlieb as "suffering through a neurotic apathy induced by the stark horror of rural Louisiana," an acerbic judgment remarkably like the ones issued by Ignatius Reilly. Nevertheless, he made friends, including a medievalist named Bob Byrne, a New Orleanian with an Irish background similar to Toole's own. Byrne was an eccentric professor given to bemoaning the fact that Western civilization, now reduced to loud popular music, tasteless movies, and vulgar literature, was crumbling.

In general, Ken Toole was gregarious, friendly, and personable, but no one absent from a gathering, friend or not, was exempt from his satirical jabs. His close friendship with a young woman who had been a fellow student at Tulane and Columbia continued, and they were even considered "unofficially engaged" until she accepted the proposal of another man. Toole seems to have been genuinely attached to her and and was considerably disturbed by her decision to end their relationship.

The summer of 1961 Ken spent in New Orleans in his parents' apartment, working on his novel. He was scheduled to return to Lafayette in the fall, but in August he was drafted and sent to boot camp. Because of his high scores on the army entrance exams and his proficiency in Spanish, he was stationed at Fort Buchanan in Puerto Rico to instruct native-speaking recruits in English. Soon he was, in his established pattern, being awarded all the army honors and medals available to him, including being named "Soldier of the Month" and a group leader, a position that entitled him to his own room. The privacy this afforded Toole, as well as the fact that his duties were not time-consuming, allowed him to make major progress on his novel. By mid-February, 1963, the protagonist had been renamed Ignatius Reilly, and on May 15 Ken wrote to his parents that the act of writing, which he had originally intended as "an attempt to seek some perspective upon the [army] situation has turned out to have been more than simple psychic therapy." He expressed the hope that he would be able to find a civilian job that would allow him time to pursue his dream: "You both know that my greatest desire is to be a writer."

By mid-August, 1963, he had been discharged and was back in New Orleans, living with his parents in the uptown area near Dominican College, a private Catholic girls' school where he had been appointed an instructor in English. Hardly had he arrived home from Puerto Rico when he presented Thelma Toole with the typescript of his unfinished novel. She read it avidly, both overwhelmed and amused by her son's faithful recreation of New Orleans settings, traditions, characters, and dialects, all of which they had observed and laughed at together through the years.

At Dominican, he taught four courses a semester, working on his novel in what little spare time he had, and in February, 1964, he typed up what he had completed and began to submit it to New York publishers. After receiving several rejections, he mailed the novel to Simon and Schuster, where it came to the attention of Gottlieb, a senior editor whose initial response was warm. For almost two years, there ensued a somewhat strange and finally, on the part of Toole, decidedly painful correspondence. The editor required substantial changes, which Toole at first willingly undertook to make. After numerous revisions, however, Gottlieb seemed to lose interest and suggested to the author that he abandon the work and attempt something new, a judgment that gravely distressed Toole. Soon, correspondence between editor and writer was broken off, and Toole seems to have abandoned writing altogether at this point.

During the next three years, he was a part-time graduate student at Tulane University, pursuing a Ph.D., and a full-time teacher at Dominican. At this point, he began to announce to friends that he wanted to be called John, not Ken. Under considerable pressure from his work and studies and the worsening situation at home—his retired father was almost totally deaf, and elocution classes had become passé, leaving Thelma unemployed and John as the family's sole provider—his demeanor and behavior underwent radical change. Surprised friends observed that the young man who had always been so attentive to his grooming and attire was sometimes unshaven, wearing unpressed suits and unpolished shoes; but more disturbing was a growing emotional instability, manifesting itself in his paranoid insistence to friends and associates that students and faculty members on both campuses were spying on him. Near the end of the fall semester of 1968, he stood up in a class at Tulane and made a speech about a plot to prevent his receiving the doctorate.

After Christmas, when the new semester began, Thelma Toole called Dominican to announce that her son was ill and would be unable to teach for a few days. After several such calls in the ensuing weeks, school administrators decided that a replacement must be hired. In fact, Thelma Toole had no idea where her son was; he had disappeared, and only later did she learn that he had been traveling somewhat aimlessly: visiting friends in Lafayette, who were shocked by his appearance and psychological condition, and as if moved by some strong compulsion, driving to various other places, including Milledgeville, Georgia, the home of the late author Flannery O'Connor and, possibly, as far as California, to visit San Simeon, the palatial home of William Randolph Hearst. In late March, 1969, police appeared at the door of the Tooles' apartment to deliver the tragic news: their son had run a hose from the exhaust pipe to the interior of his car in an isolated spot on the Mississippi Gulf Coast and brought his life to an end.

Devastated, Thelma Toole read the suicide note John Kennedy Toole had left and then destroyed it: whatever light this final written document might have shed on the young author's fatal decision would never be revealed. There began for Mrs. Toole—feeling as she did totally isolated, given her husband's deafness and the emotional distance between them that had steadily widened over the years—a long period of intense mourning during which she lost much of her mobility and was hospitalized. When her husband died, she was finally forced by her infirmity to return to the Marigny, the neighborhood of her birth and childhood, to live in the small, cramped house of her brother.

There, one morning she awoke to recall the manuscript of *A Confederacy of Dunces,* and a new phase of her life commenced as she was given purpose and strength by the desire to have the book published as a memorial to and proof of the genius she was convinced had marked her son for greatness. It was fortunate that after repeated rejections, she read of Walker Percy's class, and by an accident of fate, as it were, John Kennedy Toole's dream of becoming a recognized author was ultimately realized—alas, too late for him.

Thelma Toole, however, reveling in the posthumous fame her son acquired, made numerous public appearances. In bookstores, clubs, schools, and hospitals, she gave performances in which she played the piano, sang, recited the sad litany of the life and death of her child, and did dramatic readings from *Confederacy,* skillfully re-creating the dialects of New Orleans that John Toole had employed in the work. She even flew to New York to appear on a national late-night talk show, interspersing her familiar story with jokes about being Irish and concluding with the words "I walk in the world for my son," the motto with which she always ended any public appearance. Although she clearly relished the attention, grief for her son's death continued to haunt her, and tears were never far behind the laughter as her health declined steadily.

Two major problems remained in her life, which she must have known was drawing to a close: the proposed film version of *A Confederacy of Dunces* and the question of what to do with *The Neon Bible,* half the publication rights of which, under the convoluted and anachronistic Napoleonic code peculiar to Louisiana, belonged to his paternal uncle's heirs, who had never been close to Mrs. Toole or her son. When her efforts to persuade them to sign away their share, as they had done with *Confederacy,* failed, she determined that the earlier novel would never be published. After her death in 1984, her will revealed that she had left *The*

Neon Bible to a friend, with the understanding that it be kept from publication. As the result of a lawsuit filed by the Toole family, however, the judge ruled that if the two parties could not agree, the book would be offered at public auction. The friend to whom Mrs. Toole had bequeathed it reluctantly agreed to its publication to prevent the auction, and it was released in 1989 by Grove Press. Within two years, it had been translated into eight foreign languages, and in 1994, a British film company made a movie based on the novel.

New Orleans, although currently undergoing major changes, remains caught in a time warp, a city whose character reflects a potpourri of ethnic influences that defy any precise definition. The recent influx of industries and gambling, the "progress" fostered on the unique place by ill-advised and ill-motivated politicians, and the increased availability to its residents of information about the rest of the country and the world through various media, have left many New Orleanians unaltered and resolutely uninterested in what goes on elsewhere. Many are content, even smug, in their provincial, parochial cocoons, unable to conceive of living anywhere other than in their city or even in their own narrow neighborhood, resisting changes or "outside influences" as if they represented some fatal plague germ destined to destroy the "Big Easy." In a very real sense, this insularity has helped to preserve what is most worthwhile in the most un-American of American cities. Much of this attitude emanates from the strong Latin influence on New Orleans, which distinguishes it from any other American locale. A. J. Liebling, in a passage that serves as an epigraph for Toole's novel, insists that the "Mediterranean, Caribbean and Gulf of Mexico form a homogeneous, though interrupted sea," that New Orleans exists "within the orbit of a Hellenistic world that never touched the North Atlantic," and that it "resembles Genoa or Marseilles, or Beirut or the Egyptian Alexandria more than it does New York" (11). Surely the laid-back, "mañana" attitude of Ignatius emanates in part from this Latin lifestyle in "the City That Care Forgot." Toole is acutely sensitive to the ethnic variety of his native city, often citing in his narrative the sometimes paradoxical juxtaposition of various nationalities. For example, the Magazine Street shop at which religious "hexerei," to use Ignatius' word, are sold, is owned by Lenny, a relative of Mrs. Levy, who, as a Jew, worries about selling Catholic objects of veneration until his psychiatrist assures him that it is "kosher" to do so and he enters "some kind of exclusive agreement with a bunch of nuns who peddle the rosaries in about forty Catholic schools all over the city" (162).

Of all the New Orleans writers, John Kennedy Toole is the most typical of the city. Many came to the city from elsewhere, and those authors who were born there were, for the most part, not typical residents. George Washington Cable was an uptown Presbyterian; Lillian Hellman left the city at an early age, as did Truman Capote, whereas Toole was as irrevocably tied to New Orleans as Faulkner was to Oxford, Mississippi. No other writer, native or otherwise, seems to have *known* the city as well nor to have been able to evoke its sights and sounds and smells as powerfully as he. So accurate is his portrayal that the one major error he makes concerning the city—the narrator describes "the sun beginning to descend over the Mississippi at the foot of Canal Street" (14), which is east of the city, not west—comes as a shock to the local reader.

Ignatius Reilly, the bloated, Gargantuan, and malcontented protagonist of *A Confederacy of Dunces,* is clearly possessed of this solipsistic view of the place of his birth in which he has spent all of his days, venturing beyond the city limits on only one occasion, when he rides the Greyhound Scenicruiser to Baton Rouge: "Outside of the city limits, the heart of darkness, the true wasteland begins" (22). With this denunciation of everything beyond the boundaries of New Orleans, Toole's protagonist is only expressing a sentiment common to a large percentage of the natives of his hometown. Even given his eccentricities, his devotion to the Middle Ages, Boethius, and Fortuna—subjects of which the average New Orleanian is now, was then, and will in all likelihood always remain blissfully unaware—Ignatius embodies an entire complex of traits that I would identify as constituting a sort of generic New Orleans character. In his journal, he describes the city as "colorful and picturesque" (244) and as "a comfortable metropolis which has a certain apathy and stagnation which I find inoffensive" (131), and he fantasizes about the existence of "aristocratic Creole scholars" (261) who will come to his defense when he is attacked. With the typical contempt of the New Yorker for less "sophisticated" areas of the country, Myrna Minkoff, in a letter to Ignatius, urges him to leave New Orleans and condemns "the umbilical cord that binds you to that stagnant city" (92).

Ignatius does not, of course, reserve his scorn for other areas, and the criticism he freely unleashes on various aspects of the place of his birth—

the incompetence of its police, the widespread ignorance, and the rampant sensuality, particularly in the French Quarter ("an area which houses every vice that man has conceived in his wildest aberrations")—marks him as a man who belongs in and to New Orleans. It is his natural environment, a city in which eccentricity is not only tolerated but even nurtured, where residents of a particular neighborhood take pride in their distinctive and peculiar dialects, which stray far from the norm of American English in pronunciation, grammar, and usage. Even Ignatius' puritanical outbursts against the Quarter, with its "degenerates and wrecks and drifters," is typical of those who dwell in other areas of New Orleans, many of whom would readily allow bulldozers and wreckers to level the Vieux Carré, even though its ability to attract tourists provides the major source of municipal income.

The enthusiastic reception accorded *Confederacy of Dunces* by readers in New Orleans is somewhat surprising, since a large percentage of its residents are not particularly interested in literature. Most novels, short stories, and plays written in and about the city are read by only a small segment of the population who might be referred to as an "intellectual elite." Yet local interest in *Confederacy* cuts across class and educational lines, remarkable because New Orleanians tend to bristle at any adverse criticism of that favorite topic, their hometown. That Toole, without hesitation, points out the city's faults, and that he caustically satirizes many of its time-honored traditions, its people, its peculiar corruption of the English language, might have been thought a deterrent to local enjoyment (as was the case with Faulkner, among other "prophets" who were without honor only in their own land). Amazingly, however, New Orleanians seem rather to relish the negative aspects of the city enumerated in *Confederacy,* for example, Ignatius' pietistic denunciation of it as a "flagrant vice capital . . . famous for its gamblers, prostitutes, exhibitionists, anti-Christs, alcoholics, sodomites, drug addicts, fetishists, onanists, pornographers, frauds, jades, litterbugs, and lesbians" (15). Within its pages, local readers are not deterred from reveling in the recognition of those elements of life in the city that strike them as familiar.

What exactly do New Orleanians like about the novel? They are, I believe, amused and bemused by the author's grasp of and credible representation of local customs—social, ethical, and culinary—and his ability, probably a gift from his mother, for identifying qualities that distinguish residents of particular neighborhoods and for capturing their voices. Thus for natives, reading *A Confederacy of Dunces* becomes a uniquely personal experience; from the moment when, in the very first paragraph, they discover the unlikely hero "waiting under the clock at the D. H. Holmes department store"—for years, a favorite meeting place for shoppers in the downtown area—the native knows he is on familiar ground. The authentic portrayal of life in the city provides a pleasure distinct from that of the non-native. Frequently, I have heard New Orleanians, young or old, professors and students, executives and workmen, insist that readers from elsewhere could not possibly appreciate Toole's achievement. "How could anyone not *from* here understand?" they ask, almost jealously guarding what they see as peculiarly their own, citing characters such as Santa Battaglia or Officer Mancuso. Several New Orleanians have informed me with conviction that they know the person on whom this or that character—Irene Reilly, Santa, Miss Trixie, Burma Jones, or Gus Levy, for example—was based. One peculiar legend that developed around the book—New Orleans is, of course, a city in love with its myths, mysteries, and fantasies—involves a belief that it was actually written by Walker Percy, although anyone familiar with *The Moviegoer* or *The Last Gentleman* can clearly see that, although philosophically and religiously the two writers are much akin, the characters and situations are alien to Percy's style.

John Kennedy Toole's Ignatius Reilly represents some of the quirkiest but most prevalent qualities of New Orleans natives. His refusal to leave the city, for example, until threatened with imminent incarceration in a mental ward seems not at all peculiar to the average resident, who cannot imagine life in any other clime, certainly not in that "heart of darkness," New York City. New Orleans natives are the most provincial and chauvinistic, the most insular and solipsistic residents in the country, with the possible exception of Bostonians or Texans. Possessed of boundless unwillingness to acknowledge any serious faults in their hometown or to do anything other than praise it, they are fond of boasting of certain records, most of questionable virtue and veracity: that New Orleanians drink more coffee and liquor and eat more bread per capita than people anywhere else in the country; that the city has more churches and bars than any other American city; and other distinctions, which, they seem to believe, not only make the place distinct but also glorious.

New Orleans is, however, not only provincial but also singularly parochial. The discrete and unique neighborhoods, originally established

Bronze statue of Ignatius Reilly "waiting under the clock" at the
D. H. Holmes department store in New Orleans
Photo by W. Kenneth Holditch

along ethnic lines, may have lost some of their identifying anomalies in the past twenty-five years, but the separation still exists. Each of the neighborhoods—the French Quarter, the Faubourg Marigny, the Garden District, the Irish Channel, Bywater, and Gentilly, for example—not only has its own identity but also survives in a remarkable kind of isolation, its residents often disdaining those who live in other areas. In New Orleans, people tenaciously *identify* with their part of the city, scorning all other districts. All these neighborhood names, each carrying its own specific connotations of status and class, are still employed freely and often by residents.

No writer has ever known these distinctions or portrayed them with such realistic detail as Toole. Only George Washington Cable approaches to any degree the accuracy of Toole's grasp of the city's compartmental nature. In his essay "New Orleans as a Literary Center," published in *Literary New Orleans,* Lewis P. Simpson credits Walker Percy and John Kennedy Toole with having rescued New Orleans, to some degree, from "its imprisonment in the exotic mode."[3] In the past, authors have traditionally concentrated their attention on two areas of the city: the French Quarter and, to a lesser extent, the Garden District. Percy and Toole expand the focus of their interest to include some of the other distinctive neighborhoods that contribute much to making New Orleans unique. In his introduction to *Confederacy,* Percy acknowledges the extent to which Toole accomplished this, observing that one significant virtue of the work "is his rendering of the particularities of New Orleans, its back streets, its out-of-the-way neighborhoods, its odd speech." This approach, Percy notes, includes a portrayal of the city's "ethnic whites" and of Burma Jones, "in whom Toole has achieved the near impossible, a superb character of immense wit and resourcefulness without the least trace of Rastus minstrelsy" (8).

In the course of the narrative, Ignatius moves through many of the major New Orleans neighborhoods. In the French Quarter, "that sinkhole of vice," a modern "Sodom and Gomorrah" (221–22), Ignatius navigates his Paradise Vendor's cart along the "old flagstone banquettes" (280) of St. Peter, Royal, and Chartres Streets and Pirate's Alley. The Reillys live in a "miniature house" (369) on Constantinople Street near Tchoupitoulas, in the Irish Channel, an uptown community settled by immigrant laborers brought to the South from the East Coast in the late 1800s to dig canals. Ignatius acknowledges his Irish heritage when he boasts that "I am not without an innate sense of rhythm; my ancestors must have been rather outstanding at jigging on the heath" (133). His mother had grown up on Dauphine Street in the Seventh Ward, a district she remembers as being tough and difficult. Driving along St. Charles Avenue to the Reilly house, Detective Mancuso observes the "ancient oaks" that arch above his head "like a canopy," smells their "moldy scent," and thinks, "in a romantic aside, that St. Charles Avenue must be the loveliest place in the world" (47–48). Carrollton, where Burma Jones drinks at Mattie's Ram-

---

3. "New Orleans as a Literary Center," in *Literary New Orleans: Essays and Meditations,* ed. Richard S. Kennedy (Baton Rouge, 1992), 82–83.

A Lucky Dog wagon in New Orleans, model for the Paradise Vendors' cart that Ignatius Reilly pushed along the streets
Photo by George Dureau

ble Inn, "is an old rural town that has even a few barns, an alienated and microcosmic village within a large city" (141). Thus the narrative displays the patchwork-quilt quality of a city still influenced strongly by its ethnic groups, each of which added its particular color to the overall pattern.

Toole inherited from his mother a talent for identifying and mimicking the various dialects of the city. The New Orleans reader immediately recognizes and even identifies with the somewhat tortured English of Irene or Santa or Burma Jones. The narrator comments of Irene's accent that it "occurs south of New Jersey only in New Orleans, that Hoboken near the Gulf of Mexico" (16). The dialogue abounds with local pronunciations and idioms, for example, "chirren" (60) and "ersters" (103), and then there are the repeated localisms in Irene's dialogue: "I wanna go wrench out my glass in the zink" (211); "Ignatius, what you done this poor man?" (377); and "I just bought them fresh this morning over by Magazine Street" (51). (A recent headline in the New Orleans *Times-Picayune* contains the same misuse of *by* for another preposition, as in the last example: ONE DEAD, ONE HURT/IN SHOOTING BY XAVIER.) The juxtaposition of Ignatius' arcane vocabulary and his euphuistic bombast—he characterizes a Board of Health inspector as "that obvious appendage of officialdom" (218), describes his hot-dog peddling as being "connected in a most vital manner with the food merchandising industry" (195), and imagines Myrna lying in "the bed of some Eurasian existentialist" (397)—with the localisms intensifies the humor of the novel.

There are, in addition, references to specific New Orleans places (St. Louis Cathedral, Maison Blanche and D. H. Holmes department stores, Charity Hospital, Eads Plaza, the Roosevelt Hotel, the Algiers ferry ramp, the Prytania Theatre, three-story townhouses and shotgun doubles), events (Mardi Gras and the Pirate's Alley art show), local characters (the pirate Jean Lafitte and the black woman who "sells them pralines in front the cemetery") (227), food (stuffed eggplants, jambalaya, Dr. Nut, and "odors of Mediterranean cooking" floating out of windows) (277), and other elements unique to the city (the Desire bus, which in 1948 replaced the more famous streetcar of the same name, and the Crescent City Democrats and the Old Regulars, two political organizations). One character cogently observes that what is "so wonderful about New Orleans" is that "you can masquerade and Mardi Gras all year round if you want to. Really sometimes the Quarter is like one big costume ball" (268).

Another element that identifies Ignatius as New Orleans born and bred is the esoteric nature of his religious views. Some aspects of New Orleans Catholicism represent a bizarre, exotic transformation of traditional orthodoxy, quite distinct from the Roman religion as practiced in any other American city. Numerous factors have contributed to impart to the church Caribbean and Mediterranean overtones. There is, first of all, the proximity of the city to Central and South America, which has resulted in something akin to a banana-republic mentality, a phenomenon

Statue of St. Expedite in Our Lady of Guadalupe Church, a dubious saint,
whose name perhaps derives from the crate in which it was shipped
from Italy, marked "Expedite"
Photo by W. Kenneth Holditch

that A. J. Liebling and Walker Percy have examined in detail. In addition, there is the unique demographic history of the city: founded by the French, it provided sanctuary for thousands of Creoles fleeing from the West Indies slave rebellions at the end of the eighteenth century, absorbed a large influx of Italian, Sicilian, and Irish immigrants in the late 1800s, and, in the wake of other revolutions and wars of this century, became home for countless Latin American refugees.

What emerged from this unusual amalgamation of cultures was a religion heavily tinged with elements of non-Catholic rituals, including voodoo. Some Italians in the city are so strongly devoted to St. Joseph that his feast day is still celebrated as in Sicily, with the construction of large altars laden with traditional foods and a parade through the streets during which fava beans are thrown to the crowd. It is not unusual for those wishing to sell a piece of property to bury a statue of St. Joseph upside down in the yard, and at Our Lady of Guadalupe church there is a statue of St. Expedite, unknown outside New Orleans. This saint, who may owe his existence, some historians believe, to the fact that the crate in which the statue was shipped from Italy was stamped with instructions to "expedite," is widely venerated in the city.

Toole makes rich use of this arcane religious atmosphere in various references: St. Odo of Cluny parish, the Fisherman's Mass, raffles of rosaries and outboard motors by nuns, Santa Battaglia's mantel shrine to her mother's memory, her picture of the Infant Jesus of Prague, and the statue of "Our Lady of the Television," attached to her set by a suction cup. Irene recalls fondly the holy pictures Ignatius won as a child in parochial school, buys "a nice little pair of beads filled with Lourdes water" for her neighbor who is ill, and when disturbed by Officer Mancuso's troubles, insists that they must all "say a rosary for the police force" (19). At Levy Pants, where he sets up a statue of St. Anthony, Ignatius foments rebellion among the black factory workers and prays to St. Martin de Porres, the "patron saint of mulattoes" (139). In an anonymous note he warns Dr. Talc that St. Cassian of Imola was killed with a stylus by his students (140).

A self-proclaimed anachronism, "a seer and philosopher cast into a hostile century" (300), Ignatius is medieval not only in his peculiar religious tenets and practices but also in his secular existence. He professes to scorn "lanolin, cellophane, plastic, television, and subdivisions," fluorescent tubes, and other modern "perversions," even while his actions contradict his words: he watches television, goes to the movies, and devours frozen TV dinners. Convinced as he is that "with the breakdown of the Medieval system, the gods of Chaos, Lunacy, and Bad Taste gained ascendancy" (40), and unalterably opposed to "the relativism of modern Catholicism" and to "the current Pope," he represents a medieval Catholic practicing a religion little altered by the passage of the past five or six hundred years. Even the bubonic plague he sees as a "valid Medieval fate" (112), and he regrets having to live in "this brutal century" (390) when "martyrdom is meaningless" (61). He mourns the loss of "theology and geometry," which characterized the medieval world as he views it, and finds the absence of these elements to be demonstrated in odd ways; for example, the fact that the delinquent teenager George's tight trousers "bulged offensively at the crotch" (173) represents a violation of those medieval truths.

Scornful of Protestants and their music—"spirituals and those deadly nineteenth-century Calvinist hymns" (136)—he tells the black laborers at Levy Pants that they would be happier in the Middle Ages and conceives of his campaign with Gays and Lesbians as a "medieval Morality play. Pragmatism and Morality spar in the boxing ring of my brain" (282). He plays the lute, venerates Hroswitha, a "sybil of a medieval nun" (259), idolizes Boethius, a Roman whose *Consolation of Philosophy* was "the very basis for medieval thought" (172), and, like Boethius, cites the goddess Fortuna to explain the good and bad experiences of life. While Ignatius was in high school, his dog Rex died, and according to Irene, he "goes over to the priest and ax him to come say something over the dog" (371). When the priest refused, Ignatius conducted his own ceremony, burying the dog in the front yard under a Celtic cross, and abandoned the Catholic church. Only under duress from his mother does he attend services, and on one such rare visit, he collapses and falls into the aisle during a sermon on sloth. His prayers are offered up to arcane ancients such as Mathurin, "the patron saint of clowns" (240), to whom he directs a petition for Mr. Clyde, his employer at Paradise Vendors. For relief of his own unique intestinal disorders, he invokes St. Medericus; and for his mother, whom he believes to be an alcoholic, "I sent a prayer flying to St. Zita of Lucca, who spent her life as a house servant and practiced many austerities" (241). When, at the conclusion of the novel, Myrna Minkoff comes to New Orleans just in time to save Ignatius from incarceration in the mental ward of Charity Hospital, she describes him in his womblike bedroom as "this strange medieval mind in its cloister" (401). Ignatius is, in short, a compendium of oddities, a fact that he acknowledges, perhaps unwittingly, when he professes that "my being has many facets" (266).

Not only are the characters religious in a way that is peculiar to New Orleanians, but even the tone of the narrative is filled with religious imagery. For example, Lana Lee, owner of the Night of Joy bar on Bourbon Street, counting the money she has made from the sale of pornographic photographs for which she posed, is described as making sounds "like the imprecations of a priestess":

> Whispered numerals and words floated upward from her coral lips. . . . Her fine body, itself a profitable investment through the years, bent reverently over the formica top altar. Smoke, like incense, rose from the cigarette in the ashtray at her elbow, curling upward with her prayers, up above the host which she was elevating in order to study the date of its minting, the single silver dollar that lay among the offerings. Her bracelet tinkled, calling communicants to the altar, . . . An offering fell to the floor, the host, and Lana knelt to venerate and retrieve it. (85)

The only other person in the "temple" to witness this secular and materialistic sacrament is Burma Jones, but having been "excommunicated from the Faith because of his parentage" (85), he continues to half-heartedly mop the floor.

It is important to note that although *A Confederacy of Dunces* is not autobiographical and John Kennedy Toole is not Ignatius, nor is his mother in any way like Irene Reilly, the author drew heavily on his background for the novel. Certainly, in the character of Ignatius there are elements of Toole himself, of his mother, and of his friend Bob Byrne, but no single person constitutes the prototype of that gargantuan protagonist—indeed, could any one person fill such a monumental role? What the author achieved in the work, among other things, is much more than a powerful evocation of one of America's most uniquely fascinating cities—it is what Walker Percy calls a "*commedia*," a label that, of course, evokes a comparison to Dante. Through the power of his satirical but accepting humor, John Kennedy Toole has created a powerful religious statement that at the same time entertains readers worldwide, many of them unaware that they are, as with the novels of Walker Percy, being preached to.

At the conclusion of *A Confederacy of Dunces*, Ignatius is on his way to New York City with Myrna Minkoff, leaving behind him the havoc he has wreaked in his home and at Levy Pants as he proclaims, "I must go flower in Manhattan" (398). It is interesting to speculate what might have happened to this bizarre figure in a city so alien to his own, and, indeed, many readers have wondered whether or not Toole, had he lived, would have written a sequel. Perhaps Ignatius would have flowered in alien soil, but it seems unlikely.

During the few years between the publication of the novel and her death, Mrs. Toole was contacted, by mail, by phone, and in person, by numerous and varied fans of her son's work, many of them with projects for which they sought her imprimatur. One of the most bizarre of several bizarre propositions was that advanced by a man who wanted to write the sequel: *Ignatius in New York*. Mrs. Toole heard him out but wisely rejected the idea on the grounds that only her son could have written such a book. It was wise as well, surely, because between Ignatius Reilly and the city of New Orleans there exists a symbiotic relationship out of which grew most of the humor and the magic of this remarkable and incomparable piece of fiction.

Shirley Ann Grau
Photo by Jerry Bauer

Roadwalker in the Magic Kingdom:
Shirley Ann Grau

THOMAS J. RICHARDSON

Shirley Ann Grau's connections to New Orleans seem to be well established. She was born in the Crescent City in 1929, and she graduated from high school at Ursuline Academy. Her college years were spent at Sophie Newcomb, where she finished in 1950 and where she edited *Carnival,* the campus literary magazine in which her first stories appeared. Her early writing for *Holiday* magazine was about New Orleans society and included features on Mardi Gras and Galatoire's restaurant. She married James Feibleman, the chair of the philosophy department at Tulane, in 1955, and she and her family have continued to live part time in Metairie. Much of her best-known fiction is set in New Orleans, including *The House on Coliseum Street* (1961) and *The Condor Passes*

(1971), as well as several excellent short stories in *The Black Prince* (1954), *The Wind Shifting West* (1973), and *Nine Women* (1986). Her most recent novel, *Roadwalkers* (1994), is set largely in New Orleans.[1]

Thus Grau's ties to New Orleans are deep and abiding. Yet her life and work are not completely focused there. As all of her biographers note, she also lived as a child in Montgomery, Alabama, where her father had connections and where she studied classics at the Booth School. Most of her first stories collected in *The Black Prince* focus on African American characters in the rural South or on the Gulf Coast, outside New Orleans. Grau's best-known and most highly regarded novel, *The Keepers of the House* (1964), for which she won a Pulitzer Prize, is set in the rural South somewhere between New Orleans and Atlanta (both cities are mentioned in the story), and her first novel, *The Hard Blue Sky* (1958), is set on an island off the Louisiana coast. As her family has grown, she has divided her time between her home in Metairie and a summer home on Martha's Vineyard, a world where a number of her later stories in *The Wind Shifting West* and *Nine Women* are set. If a large part of *Roadwalkers* is set in New Orleans, an equally significant part is set elsewhere—in the rural South during the Depression, where homeless children wander alone, and in a boarding school for young women outside the South.

Naturally, perhaps, critical commentary on Grau has taken the importance of New Orleans in her work for granted. Paul Schlueter, the author of the Twayne book on Grau (1981), says in his essay in *Fifty Southern Writers After 1900* that Grau is "a regional writer akin to Sarah Orne Jewett and Willa Cather, not a writer who uses 'Southern' atmosphere, characters and settings for superficial local color narratives." In the essay collection *Louisiana Women Writers,* Elzbieta Olesky focuses on *The Keepers of the House,* comparing it to *Gone with the Wind.* In probably the best single essay on Grau's work, "Shirley Ann Grau's Wise Fictions," Linda Wagner-Martin surveys the broad thematic concerns of Grau's work in relation to the contexts of the book in which her essay appears—*Southern Women Writers: The New Generation.* She points out, quite rightly, a variety of ways in which Grau's work is defined by her understanding of women's lives, especially as these women relate to the "patri-

---

1. All of Shirley Ann Grau's works of fiction were published by Alfred A. Knopf, New York. Page references for quotations are inserted parenthetically in the text.

archal matrix that seems to dominate Southern life."[2] In addition, she suggests that Grau's consistent concern with nonwhite culture is set against patriarchal southern life as well.

Wagner-Martin's sense of profound contrasts in Grau's work is correct, and those contrasts seem to extend beyond the theme of women versus patriarchy. Certainly, the conflicts—between men and women, blacks and whites—are the place to start, but they can be expanded. For example, as Anthony Bukoski has noted, the presence of houses and homes in Grau's stories provides insight into her fiction, but those houses and the shelter they represent are defined against the wanderers, as in *Roadwalkers,* or in Grau's repeated motif of "a man outside," where a vagrant or thief stands outside various houses and is seen by the people inside.[3] Another noticeable contrast in Grau's work is between the rich and the poor. If her early work is concerned with primitive characters, as in *The Black Prince* and *The Hard Blue Sky,* then much of her later work in *The Wind Shifting West* and *Evidence of Love* focuses on the wealthy, and both *A Condor Passes* and *Roadwalkers* offer main characters who move from being very poor to being very rich.

The contrast in Grau's own biography between her lives in New Orleans and in Montgomery is apparent, but the contrasts offered the artist within New Orleans culture itself are extreme. Lewis P. Simpson has speculated on why reasonably few writers stayed in New Orleans long term (Whitman, Dos Passos, Anderson, Faulkner, among others); he thought that perhaps New Orleans was so far removed from the reality of living in America that it offered no enduring metaphor for the American writer—that it was too exotic.[4] In my work, I have suggested that the vivid contrast between "the city of day" and "the city of night" was stimu-

---

2. Paul Schlueter, "Shirley Ann Grau," in *Fifty Southern Writers After 1900,* ed. Joseph M. Flora and Robert Bain (New York, 1987), 225; Elzbieta Olesky, "Keepers of the House: Scarlett O'Hara and Abigail Howland," in *Louisiana Women Writers: New Essays and a Comprehensive Bibliography,* ed. Dorothy Brown and Barbara Ewell (Baton Rouge, 1992), 169–82; Linda Wagner-Martin, "Shirley Ann Grau's Wise Fictions," in *Southern Women Writers: The New Generation,* ed. Tonnette B. Inge (Tuscaloosa, Ala., 1990), 145.

3. Anthony Bukoski, "The Burden of Home: Shirley Ann Grau's Fiction," *Critique,* XXVII (1987), 181–93.

4. Lewis P. Simpson, "New Orleans as a Literary Center: Some Problems," in *Literary New Orleans,* ed. Richard S. Kennedy (Baton Rouge, 1992), 76–88.

lating to Tennessee Williams, and the exotic quality of New Orleans set against its materialism was useful to his work. In viewing New Orleans as a city of differences, one might contrast the Vieux Carré with the Garden District, or the tourist culture with housing projects. One might also note the contrasts in New Orleans history—comparing the Creole culture before the Louisiana Purchase to American society after 1803—or set Mardi Gras high society against the homeless wanderers in the streets around Jackson Square. Or one might note the fantasy of Bourbon Street at midnight (a world that escapes time) as well as the reality of the same street in the early morning light (a world in which aged buildings and decaying signs show the ravages of time).

Grau's preoccupation with aging and death in her various stories extends the sense of history and time in New Orleans. In her introduction to George Washington Cable's *Old Creole Days*, Grau notes especially Cable's interest in the mutability and transience of the old Creole community, as well as his insight into its self-destructive pride. Many of Grau's own characters are overtly self-destructive in much the same way some Creoles were, bringing families and communities down with them, others defining themselves as women alone, set against the culture and time.

A brief survey of Grau's New Orleans work should begin with her early travel pieces for *Holiday*, continue with "Miss Yellow Eyes" from *The Black Prince*, focus on *The House on Coliseum Street* and *The Condor Passes*, comment on "The Thieves" and "Stanley" in *The Wind Shifting West*, and conclude with "The Beginning" in *Nine Women* and its extension into *Roadwalkers*, where Grau attempts to bring some reconciliation to her world of contrasts and her sense of time.

Grau wrote several pieces for *Carnival*, but she says that the writing she produced for *Holiday* in the mid-1950s offered her experience and money. Among several articles that featured houses on the Mississippi River and scenes on the Mississippi Gulf Coast, two focus on New Orleans and indicate that Grau not only knows the city intimately but has an "inside"perception of society. The first of these discusses the merits of Galatoire's restaurant, especially its appeal to New Orleans folk. The descriptions of Galatoire's history, atmosphere, and food are interwoven with family anecdotes about Grau's uncle, who has eaten at Galatoire's "once or twice a week for fifty years." Grau notes the recent influx of tourists: "An old woman in her seventies, tall, thin, and very much the lady, who has been going to Carnival balls since she was fifteen and can tell you the name of every queen of Comus for the last half-century . . . laments that you can go into Galatoire's and not see one person that you know." A later article depicts New Orleans society in Mardi Gras season. Grau describes the Mardi Gras social whirl as experienced by the young and beautiful Queen of Rex, but she also notes the strong family traditions associated with the balls and the parades. For the young queen, "today was the triumph of her life"as a debutante, and she not only remembers dreaming of Mardi Gras as a child but knows too that her grandmother had been carnival royalty and her great-grandfather as well. Accompanying the article are pictures of the cream of New Orleans society, but Grau also notes the "seamy underside"of Mardi Gras. In addition, in a manner reminiscent of Cable, Gayarré, or Grace King, she mentions the carnival activities of the New Orleans Creoles, those descendants of early French and Spanish settlers who "are acutely aware that they are descendants of a brilliant, dashing group." Now, however, time and lack of money has "left them little more than memories."[5]

Among Grau's early stories in *The Black Prince,* the only one with a clear New Orleans setting is "Miss Yellow Eyes." It is among her best stories of racial conflict. Told by Celia, the fourteen-year-old black sister of Lena, a girl with golden eyes who can pass for white, the story tells of Lena's romance with another light-skinned black, Chris, and their plans to move to Oregon, where they can "become" white. Their plans are destroyed when Chris is killed in Korea and Lena is left to cope with her dark-complexioned brother, Pete, a militant black who belongs to an all-black club with a sign on the door that reads "white entrance to rear." Grau's use of colors in this story is detailed by Paul Schlueter, but the contrasts in the story are clear. The background of racial complexity in New Orleans is well known, given the history of quadroons and *les gens de couleur libre.* In "Miss Yellow Eyes," all avenues lead to despair. Not only is Lena left alone after Chris's death, but Pete, who loses his arm in a switchyard accident, becomes increasingly violent and bitter about Lena and Pete's hopes. In Pete's eyes, Chris has died for nothing, just as their own father had died in an earlier war. Schlueter also notes the religious overtones of death, sacrifice, and names in "Miss Yellow Eyes," but

5. Shirley Ann Grau, "Galatoire's of New Orleans," *Holiday,* XX (October, 1956), 66; Grau, "New Orleans Society," *Holiday,* XXIII (March, 1958), 119.

the racial complexity and contradictions in the story are inextricably connected to New Orleans community and history. Here is a nineteenth-century quadroon story set in the mid-twentieth century, in which no sentiment or happy ending is possible.

Much of the critical commentary on Grau's first novel, *The Hard Blue Sky,* and on the early stories in *The Black Prince,* pictures Grau as a "fictional anthropologist," a distant observer, perhaps even callous in her depiction of the forces of nature and of the primitive people who struggle to survive in a violent world. According to Ann Pearson, in Grau's work "nature is the vision." Such commentary might apply as well to *The House on Coliseum Street,* one of Grau's best-known New Orleans novels, in which her objectivity is, as Chester Eisinger suggests, "little short of chilling." As Linda Wagner-Martin points out, *The House on Coliseum Street* emphasizes the "ravages of time" with its seasonal structure: June, End of Summer, The House on Coliseum Street, and Winter.[6] Joan Mitchell's affair with one of her sister's boyfriends is followed by an abortion on the Mississippi Coast, then her obsessive behavior after the abortion as she returns to the house on Coliseum Street, where her family has lived for generations. Joan is indeed a "woman alone" as she rejects the various members of her family and friends around her—her sister Doris; her mother, who has been married five times and has a daughter by each husband; her suitor, Fred Aleman, who would marry her at any time; and finally Michael Kern, whose career she destroys by reporting their affair and the abortion to the dean at the local university. Her settled life on Coliseum Street was hardly settled, given the nature of her mother's family (the last husband still lives alone in the attic), but it is clearly shattered by the abortion and the events that ensue.

On the morning of her first phone call from Michael, Joan observes an aging wino stumble into Coliseum Street and sees the "street close up on itself" before the police come to pick him up. A harbinger, perhaps, but of what? Men, aging, time? Standing where the tramp stood, Joan will remember this event at the end of the story, and she will compare the fact that he disappeared, leaving no trace, to the baby she has lost—"there wasn't anything left of it" (241). When she sees the tramp for the first

6. Ann Pearson, "Shirley Ann Grau: Nature Is the Vision," *Critique,* XVIII (1975), 47; Chester Eisinger, "Grau, Shirley Ann," in *Contemporary Novelists,* ed. James Vinson (New York, 1972), 515; Wagner-Martin, "Shirley Ann Grau's Wise Fictions," in *Southern Women Writers,* ed. Inge, 148.

time, she is looking at him from the security of her bedroom, twenty feet up on the second floor. As the book ends, Joan returns to the house, and while she is locked out in the early morning hours, she identifies herself as the owner of the house, the oldest child, the one with money, but it is a slight victory in the face of her anger, loneliness, and self-destruction. In Walker Percy's *The Moviegoer,* a novel published the same year as *The House on Coliseum Street,* Binx Bolling faces the existential dilemma posed by the meaninglessness of modern existence, but he has the contexts of southern stoicism and Catholicism as guides, and he has a healthy sense of the absurd. *The House on Coliseum Street* is a much darker book, and the ending offers little hope, in spite of Joan's fetal position and what we assume will be a new life for her.

Grau's next book, *The Keepers of the House,* establishes a stronger link between the generations of a family in the rural South and the property that they hold. Again, there is the broad theme of destruction related to miscegenation in the family that is not entirely resolved by the young woman who becomes "the keeper" at story's end. She is, certainly, a much stronger and less self absorbed character than Joan Mitchell, and her concerns are wider, in keeping with the novel's multigenerational story of southern history of which she is a part.

The Condor Passes has not been as highly regarded as *The Keepers of the House,* but the story it tells about aging, the disintegration of a wealthy family, and the destructive effects of money is readable enough that it qualified as a Book-of-the-Month Club selection. It is largely set in New Orleans and, as various critics have pointed out, has been unfairly compared to Mario Puzo's *The Godfather,* published two years earlier. Grau's story focuses on the Mafia-like empire of a New Orleans crime boss, his rise to power from poverty, and his influence on his family and estate, even as a ninety-five-year-old man. In his book on Grau, Schlueter quotes Grau as saying that you can't live in New Orleans and not know many Italian families who've made it big with a start as rumrunners (70). Grau tells the story from multiple perspectives, a technique that she used successfully in *The Keepers of the House.* The first section, "Stanley," is told from the point of view of a black valet who has grown wealthy working for "the old man." As it turns out, the black condor (the symbol of the estate) is associated not only with the old man's death but also with Stanley, especially in the setting of the aviary and greenhouse that opens and closes the book. At the end of the story, Stanley is seen as the condor, with arms that flutter like wings, when the old man dies. Stanley's point of view is useful in describing the family, its wealth, and especially the power of the old man, and his section of the story is reprinted, in a different form, as a story in *The Wind Shifting West*.

The second section, "The Old Man," tells us more about Thomas Henry Oliver and his rise from poverty to immense wealth. Born poor in a river town in Ohio, he leaves at age thirteen and makes money immediately in small-time crime—as a burglar, pickpocket, pimp. He went to sea at seventeen, "dealt with everything that could be smuggled," and is faithful in sending his mother substantial money. He comes to New Orleans after jumping ship in the coastal marsh to escape smallpox, and he soon builds his empire through interests in gambling, real estate, and bootlegging. After his marriage into a respectable family, his family expands to include two daughters, Anna and Margaret, and a Cajun boy, Robert, whom he grooms to be his successor and son-in-law. However, the broad pattern of the novel is not to emphasize the world of wealth/society/respectability versus the world of crime/poverty/violence, though such clearly exists both in the novel and in New Orleans. The strength of the old man is that he has been able to bridge the gap, to revel in the life of the streets while he amasses his fortune. As noted earlier, however, the emphasis in *The Condor Passes* is on destruction of the various members of Oliver's family, and the various sections of the novel show their individual disintegration. The family, then, will not continue to future generations. The old man's powers are great but shallow, and time and age bring him to a vision of the condor, the bird of death. *The Condor Passes* shows us that Grau knows quite well the patterns of time and history in the Big Easy.

Wagner-Martin notes that "the immensity of the cultural forces displayed in *The Keepers of the House* in this novel reach only to Robert's perversity, Anna's self-centeredness, and Margaret's insatiable appetites."[7] In comparison with *The Keepers of the House*, that is, *The Condor Passes* is a less substantial novel. Wagner-Martin's point is well taken, but the failure and the weakness of these characters in *The Condor Passes* is Grau's judgment on them as well as our own. In their failure she

7. Wagner-Martin, "Shirley Ann Grau's Wise Fictions," in *Southern Women Writers,* ed. Inge, 156.

demonstrates something of the modern world's perversity, certainly as she sees it in New Orleans.

The Wind Shifting West includes one story clearly set in New Orleans, "The Thieves," as well as "Stanley," a different version of the black valet section in *The Condor Passes*. "The Other Way" is a school desegregation story that focuses on a Cajun French-speaking black family, but whether it is set in New Orleans or some other part of Louisiana is not clear. "The Thieves," set in the French Quarter, tells about a young woman trapped by loneliness. Her parents have returned to Sicily, and her lover, Steve, is a suitor of empty promise. In the action of the story, she spots a burglar in the courtyard below her window, hiding from the police, and she spontaneously whispers to him the way of escape. Later, when Steve arrives to tell her that he is marrying someone else but hopes to continue their relationship, she is able to dismiss him. As Schlueter points out, she realizes that the silence was no emptier after he had left than it had been with him there.[8] Here is another of Grau's women alone. Sheltered, perhaps, in one world, she sees the predicament of the burglar in the other, "street" world below. By helping him, she somehow finds new strength. His escape from the police parallels her own move to freedom. In *The Wind Shifting West,* various women, old and young, are faced with problems that focus on their loneliness and the conflicts of one world impinging on another.

Evidence of Love is an extended version of "The Patriarch," a story in *The Wind Shifting West*. According to Jean Ross, it is a story of "rootlessness" that is set in several places, all outside the South. She sees it as "losing touch with the Southern settings and characters which are the strengths of Grau's best writing."[9] Again, though, the broad problems of aging and time are much in evidence here, as they are in New Orleans stories. Here, the aging male who dominates the action is very much like the old man in *A Condor Passes,* given the estrangement of his "contrived" family—a son through a surrogate mother. Though the son and the father both lead self-absorbed and ineffectual lives, the daughter-in-law, Lucy, does show "evidence of love" in assisting the old man's choice to die.

8. Paul Schlueter, *Shirley Ann Grau* (Boston, 1981), 130.

9. Jean Ross, "Shirley Ann Grau," *Dictionary of Literary Biography* (Detroit, 1978), II, 213.

Nine Women includes one New Orleans story, "The Beginning," an early version of the longer story in *Roadwalkers*. The story establishes direction not only for the rest of the collection but for the novel as well—the strength and determination of women. "The Beginning" announces that the child who tells the story is seen by her mother as "the queen of the world, the jewel of the lotus, the pearl without price, my secret treasure." The mother is a wonderfully creative and talented black seamstress who gradually builds her trade among the African American community in New Orleans. The child's father was an Indian merchant, a shoe salesman, a "seller of Worthington pumps"; but the mother sees the child, and the child comes to see herself, as an Indian princess. She is the live model on which her mother's creative fashions are displayed. "The Beginning" describes the bond between mother and daughter as well as how the mother steals expensive cloth from the Perfection Cloth Shop. She opens her shop as a *modiste* in rooms above LeConte's drugstore, a "castle" complete with tower and turret.

The real beginning of the story, however, is told in *Roadwalkers,* and it reaches much farther back in the life of the mother. We learn in the opening section that the mother had been a homeless child who wandered the roads of the rural South during the 1930s, during the Great Depression. Abandoned by mother and father and left with a grandmother who died, she is the youngest of six children who struggle to survive on the road until only two are left, Baby and her brother Joseph. They survive winters, summers, days, nights, hunger, and breakbone fever. Baby is finally captured on the Aikens Grove plantation, after Joseph's anger becomes so great that he begins to destroy property and kill livestock.

In the second part of *Roadwalkers,* attention shifts to the story of the man who captures her. He is Charles Tucker, one of "the people of Clark County," the title of this section. The story of his childhood, while certainly more secure than Baby's, tells us that he is the sort of person who can understand Baby as well as the anger of her brother. He had known something of being left alone himself, before his sister took him in, and knew poverty and hard work. We are able to establish a connection between Charles Tucker and Baby, and we understand something of the larger southern world that brings these two together. In several instances, Charles is fortunate to be in the right place at the right time, as when he establishes a market for his sister's produce with a wealthy family, and in his marriage to the daughter of the manager of Aikens Grove, the position he inherits when her parents are killed. Baby turns out to be a marvelously talented fashion designer, and she does not look back to her childhood. But Grau tells us that Charles Tucker was important in her life. For once, she had the luck to be part of his good fortune.

After Charles captures Baby, he takes her to a Catholic home for children in New Orleans and assumes financial responsibility for her. This section, "The Kindness of Strangers," focuses on Rita Landry, sixteen and not yet a novice, who is given charge of the black waif brought to the convent. She is a young Acadian woman from the river country outside New Orleans. We learn briefly about her family, her mother's work for the local priest, and the mother's decision that Rita will be a nun. Rita gives Baby the name Mary Woods, and she begins the hard task of teaching her and caring for her. At first, Baby's eyes, "metallic eyes like a knife blade left out in the cold," remind Rita of eyes she had seen in caged animals at the circus. As the years pass, Rita becomes Sister Celeste, and Mary Woods expresses herself first through silent play, then through wildly extravagant and creative art. At the conclusion of this section, Mary is asked to return to Clark County to work for the household at Aikens Grove, but she disappears mysteriously from the convent. Again, as in "The People of Clark County," we see the circumstances in Rita Landry's life that bring her into the life of Mary Woods. Though Mary does not ever return to visit Sister Celeste, we establish the connection between them, as well as understand that ultimately the church does not touch Mary Woods. Her spirit had been defined much earlier, as a roadwalker.

In the sections that follow, the voice in the novel shifts and becomes that of Nanda Woods, now the thirty-six-year-old daughter of Mary Woods. The section "The Magic Kingdom" includes "The Beginning," an expanded version of the first story in *Nine Women*, and a sequel, "The Middle Kingdom." As the child model in "The Beginning," Nanda learns from her mother "the greatest enchantment of all: how to walk like a princess in kingdoms of our own making" (181). They live, she says, in two kingdoms—one a fantasy where the mother was queen and the girl was princess, the other, a reality, based on "money and property and the logic of commerce" (182). Nanda wins a scholarship to St. Catherine's, a boarding school run by the Ursuline nuns, some "832 miles about straight north of New Orleans." Nanda is black in a world of white, and to some degree, she survives because her journey there replicates the journey of her mother, the roadwalker, those many years ago. She has been taught to be a princess, and she somehow insulates herself in "the magic kingdom" against prejudice, patronizing behavior, and noblesse oblige. In *Roadwalkers,* Nanda Woods succeeds where other young black women fail. The key to her success seems to be her insulation. She knows that she is invisible to some and a symbol to others, but she maintains tight control.

After graduation, Nanda returns to New Orleans to attend college and continues to work with her mother in her shops. In the concluding section of *Roadwalkers,* "The Promised Land," both mother and daughter "arrive," so to speak: the roads that they have walked come to a kingdom that is both magical and real. The mother is financially secure. Her expensive shop, catering to whites, is elegant and successful. She marries a long-time suitor, and they buy a house in the suburbs, complete with brick barbecue, large lawn, and brand-new furniture selected by the daughter. The daughter does well at the university (Phi Beta Kappa) and meets a young black pre-med student whose father is also a doctor. They marry and settle down to a well-to-do life of travel and luxury apartments and finally, at the end, to a home in the suburbs.

What is Grau telling us here? The ending of *Roadwalkers* has been criticized by those who say it offers an easy and superficial accommodation to materialism and suburban life by two women whose early lives should make them remarkably different. Have they been roadwalkers all this distance just to come to a brick barbecue, and to come to it so easily? Any assessment of "The Promised Land" section, must not, however, be so quick to rush to pass judgment on these two women or on Shirley Ann Grau. For Grau, the mere presence of houses and marriages does not make the promised land, though they are important, as we know from the emphasis on houses and shelter throughout her work. There is more, and she knows it. The tone that pervaded Nanda's voice when she was an "invisible" student at school, or when she was her mother's princess in the magic kingdom, continues here. After Nanda completes her final exams at the end of her freshman year, she takes fried chicken and champagne and "intrudes" at the home of a white art professor at the university, where she learns once again what it means to be black in a white world. She also learns the limits of marriage, since she and her husband have both had affairs that they can "number." At the end of the novel, though, she does have a moment with her husband—"something between us, something that hovered in the air between us. A thread, frail, thin, to be measured in millimeters, but there nonetheless. For that one instant, it seemed I could see it—fine as a spider's web, shimmering with all of the colors of crystal—then it was gone. We smiled at each other, cautiously, warily, as we walked back across the worm-infested lawn" (292). So, she says, she comes into her kingdom alone.

This "moment" is a wonderful thing, one of the things in the promised land that really matter, but it is transitory, as we are made to see. In her remarks on Grau's various novels and stories before *Roadwalkers,* Linda Wagner-Martin suggests that "so much attention to the act of dying is unusual"; she is thinking especially about the aging and dying patriarchs in *The Condor Passes* and *Evidence of Love,* among others, and about patriarchy in general.[10] Grau's women, in contrast, are survivors, though they are frequently death-haunted. The "worm-infested lawn" Nanda and her husband walk across at the end of the novel is one more symbol for the roadwalker of the terms of the journey; death is ever present. Grau's promised land is material, but it is magical as well; it has to do with Nanda's understanding her own self-sufficiency in the face of death and time and how she translates her magic kingdom into reality—her "portion, neither more or less" (292).

New Orleans has a great deal to do with Grau's art beyond providing specific settings. It offers a stimulating world of contrasts—black/white, rich/poor, day/night—that are sometimes difficult to reconcile. It also juxtaposes two kingdoms, one real, with money and property, and the other a fantasy, a world of carnival and magic. As Nanda Woods realizes, however, both are "kingdoms of our own making" (181). In Grau's early New Orleans work, such as *The House on Coliseum Street* and *The Condor Passes,* her characters struggle to glimpse any magic at all. New Orleans and history, as well as the current setting, are constant reminders of the need for insight into the issues of aging, death, time, and self-destruction. Grau's use of New Orleans helps us see that all of her characters are roadwalkers, as are we, though they and we are rarely as fortunate as Nanda Woods, able to turn the magic into reality.

10. Wagner-Martin, "Shirley Ann Grau's Wise Fictions," in *Southern Women Writers,* ed. Inge, 158.

Sheila Bosworth with Walker Percy
Photo by Rhoda K. Faust, Maple Street Book Shop,
New Orleans

Latter-Day Creoles:
A New Age of New Orleans Literature

W. KENNETH HOLDITCH

When Tennessee Williams' first play destined for Broadway, *Battle of Angels,* closed ingloriously out of town after only a few performances in 1941, the playwright once again headed south to New Orleans. Recalling that episode later, he described the French Quarter as a place in which artists and writers huddled together for comfort when they had been wounded by the world; and, indeed, the old part of the city was, during the three decades before the Second World War, a haven for those struggling to establish themselves in the creative arts.

Such is, for better or worse, no longer the case, for the Vieux Carré, which held such a strong attraction for writers as an outpost of bohemia that they once flocked to the comfortable, inexpensive, and, more important, romantic shelter, has now been gentrified, customized, and over-developed by property owners and politicians determined to clean up the old courtesan, as Faulkner referred to the French Quarter in the 1920s, and make her "presentable" to the tourists, American, European, and Asian, with money to spend and, for the most part, little interest in literature. The cheap, walk-up attic flats or roach-infested rooms of the early part of this century have been replaced by time-share condos or low-ceilinged efficiency apartments where up-and-coming young lawyers and stockbrokers and art gallery owners lead a life that would no doubt seem to the struggling scribblers of Sherwood Anderson's day luxurious and lavish and sterile.

The Quarter's loss of its bohemian quality is not unique or regional, for there seem to be no more such gathering places for struggling artists in any cities; no more urban enclaves in whose garrets *la vie de Bohème* is lived in penury and maybe hunger but with enthusiasm and faith; no special bars or cafés in which aspiring novelists and poets and playwrights congregate to read each other's work-in-progress over whiskey, wine, or coffee, full of excitement and hope and willingness to sacrifice. When writers assemble nowadays, it is more likely to occur in the offices, hall-ways, or cafeterias of the universities where they teach or at the businesses for which they work, nine to five, or, if in coffeehouses or bars, during off hours from their jobs. Authors, not only in New Orleans but in other cities also, no longer live as they once did in communities nor, generally, do they hole up in cheap rooms, living on pittances, in order to complete their hoped-for masterpieces. Most writers in recent decades have held other jobs—as teachers, restaurant staff, store clerks—and have written after the workday is finished.

This is not to say, of course, that authors no longer write in New Orleans, for in truth there are probably more of them than ever before living in the city and writing about its continuing enchantment, which has, miraculously, survived the assaults of those "progressive" businessmen and politicos who would like to turn it into a copy of "progressive" cities, such as Houston or Atlanta. Although the Quarter may have been dragged, unwillingly and even unwittingly, into the twentieth century, the aura of its colorful and sometimes even lurid past still lurks in its dark corners, and numerous writers have made it their task to discover it, describe it, and preserve it. Despite the commercialization of what I term "the New Orleans literary mystique" by authors of popular romance novels, travel writers, and tourist bureaus, the mystery and romance of the city survive, though sometimes hidden beneath a veneer of the new.

That mystique is constituted of the strong and pervasive sense of foreignness that has always been part of the city, an amalgam of local color elements to which all the varied ethnic components of the population— French and Spanish settlers and, later, those of British, African, Caribbean, German, and Italian descent—have made distinctive contributions. The degree to which authors are able to encompass this exotic mixture and assimilate it realistically into their work often marks the degree to which that work is successful. In a sense, gumbo and jambalaya are ideal dishes as symbols for New Orleans because their strange combination of ingredients symbolizes well the cultural mishmash that is the city. Indeed, each ethnic group that has come to the city has added to gumbo its own element of taste, so that now the varieties of that spicy soup differ not only from neighborhood to neighborhood but even from household to household. Cooks, male and female, argue frequently about the comparative virtues of gumbo made with filé as opposed to the version made with okra, and others who produce a hybrid of the two evoke horror among natives devoted to more traditional methods. One amusing vignette drawn by Julie Smith in *New Orleans Beat* is of a woman who "looked as if she could make a lot of roux-based dishes," a comment of considerable significance in a city where interest in food borders sometimes on obsession.[1] Not surprisingly, the subject is interwoven by local authors into the narrative fabric of work after work. These writers, like the gumbo cooks, have blended the multitude of varied elements of the city to their own taste to produce remarkably distinctive creations.

Since an examination of all the contemporary authors who may truly be termed "New Orleans writers" would require a separate volume— even to list all of them would be a major undertaking—I have chosen here to focus on seven representatives of the category—three of them natives, four transplants—whose choice of subject matter, style, setting, character, and action might well be said to define what a contemporary New Orleans novel is, what might be termed a modern-day "Creole style." Two of them, Valerie Martin and Anne Rice, although quite different in their approaches, make much use of the distinctive New Orleans Gothic mode in their work. Three of them, James Lee Burke, Julie Smith,

---

1. Julie Smith, *New Orleans Beat* (New York, 1994), 329.

and Chris Wiltz, write detective or mystery novels, and two, Ellen Gilchrist and Sheila Bosworth, have produced works that may be categorized as novels of manners in the long tradition that includes Jane Austen, Henry James, and Edith Wharton.

New Orleans is a natural for the Gothic and grotesque, given its climate, its foreign quality, and certain unique facts of its history, a "*haunted* city" as an Englishman in Anne Rice's novel *The Witching Hour* describes it, where mysteries abound, some real, many imagined.[2] It is a place of ancient but ever-evolving legends and myths, emanating from several native elements: the secretive lives of the nineteenth-century Creoles; the exotic cultural traits of African slaves and West Indian immigrants; the peculiar social custom called *plaçage* and the entire structure of the *gens de couleur* society; and the existence, to whatever degree at different times, of arcane religious rituals practiced by the city's several discrete ethnic groups. Thus, Gothicism in New Orleans in many ways differs from the European tradition or that associated with other parts of the United States.

If any city in America can be said to be haunted, it is New Orleans, with its strange, dark heritage of voodoo and violence and vice. Both Anne Rice and Valerie Martin, like George Washington Cable and Lafcadio Hearn before them, make rich use of a combination of these grotesque components to enhance their fiction, each in her own way. If one stands in the Quarter on a late moonless night, surrounded by the Old World architecture (albeit prettified to suit modern urban tastes), smells of sweetness and decay, strange far-away sounds of music and voices, and an awareness of a whole world of animal life—rodents and insects—beneath every surface of wood or concrete or earth, it is possible to imagine that around the next corner, in the middle of the next block, one might encounter a vampire, a ghost, or some other grotesquerie and believe not only that the apparition is real but that somehow it is appropriate in such a place, at such a time.

Anne Rice, a native, was born uptown, in the Irish Channel, a neighborhood adjacent to but socially miles separated from the more elegant and monied Garden District. Though her family moved to Texas when she was fifteen, she never forgot the environment of her childhood, and with only a few exceptions, her books employ New Orleans as a setting

2. Anne Rice, *The Witching Hour* (New York, 1990), 3.

Anne Rice, author of *The Vampire Chronicles*
Photo by Richard S. Kennedy

for some or all of the action. Valerie Martin's family moved to the city when she was a child and most of her life has been spent there, including the formative years of childhood and early maturity during which she absorbed and assimilated those multifaceted elements that constitute the typical New Orleans lifestyle and vision. The imagined New Orleans of Martin and Rice derives much of its uniqueness from a concentration on its grotesque aspects.

Despite the romantic appeal that has resulted in its being called "America's most interesting city," there is much beneath the exotic surface that is unpleasant, corrupt, even terrifying, and although both authors acknowledge the charm and to some extent employ it, they also willingly face head-on the negative side, indeed even derive inspiration from it, employing to advantage the paradoxical amalgam that is New Orleans. Assuredly for Martin and Rice—as for George Washington

Cable (in "Jean Ah-Poquelin," for example, with its swampy setting, dark old house, and ghostly leper), Tennessee Williams (in *Suddenly Last Summer,* with its carnivorous garden), and other writers—the grotesque material integral to their work is of a homegrown variety, as far removed from various other southern Gothicisms (that of Faulkner or the Georgia school, for example) as from the New England paradigm found in Hawthorne.

No author has made more use of New Orleans than Rice, who returned to the city after fifteen years to become a writer in residence, as it were, and a permanent presence on the local literary and social scene. Most of the fourteen books she has published to date employ New Orleans as a setting to some extent, particularly the four novels in her *Vampire Chronicles* and the four concerning witchcraft, as well as *The Feast of All Saints.* In *Interview with the Vampire* and its three sequels, New Orleans is seen as it evolves over a period of two hundred years, an achievement that offers proof of thorough research of the city's history.

As a child, Rice was fascinated by the glamorous old houses, uptown and in the French Quarter, by the cemeteries and tropical vegetation, as well as by the myths and legends of a superstitious French and Sicilian and Irish populace. She recalls reading, as a child, all the literature she could find on the ghosts that supposedly inhabited various buildings around the city and having sought out haunted houses, such as the one on Melpomene Street, where local lore had it the devil lived.[3] Like many another New Orleans author, she is fascinated by the peculiar local version of Roman Catholicism, which with the many waves of immigrants took on a variety of ethnic colorations, including not only the French and Spanish, but the Caribbean, the Irish of Rice's own family, and the German, all tinged to some degree by the superstitions associated with voodoo. Like Michael Curry, a character in *The Witching Hour,* she was struck as a child by the remarkable fact that because of the animosity among different groups of immigrants, one uptown neighborhood contained two Catholic churches, built across the street from each other, one Irish, one German.

Rice repeatedly employs a multitude of indigenous Gothic touches— for example, the decay resulting from the damp climate, the rank under-

3. The comments and observations attributed to Anne Rice in this essay are taken from a series of interviews and conversations between her and the author over the past fifteen years.

growth of an almost tropical vegetation, and the abundance of insects and rodents—to provide an appropriate backdrop for her supernatural beings. In *The Witching Hour,* the doctor's strong impressions of the Garden District mansion, based on Rice's own residence at the time, is of the smell of "heat and old wood" and of omnipresent and troubling decay: "Spiders wove their tiny intricate webs over the iron lace roses. In places the iron had so rusted that it fell away to powder at the touch" (5). When at the end of *Interview with the Vampire* Louis returns home after a lengthy sojourn in Europe, he finds New Orleans much changed but still recognizable, "as if the very air were perfumed and peculiar there."[4] Similarly, Rice, during her many years of what she termed "exile" in San Francisco, experienced a keen hunger for the overpowering sense impressions—sights and sounds and smells, taste and touch—that characterize New Orleans in her memory, imagination, and on the pages of her novels.

In her second novel, *The Feast of All Saints,* it is neither vampires nor witches that concern Rice, but Creoles of color in the decades before the Civil War. No aspect of New Orleans history is more exotic or less publicized than *plaçage,* the system under which white Creole men, generally though not exclusively those of French or Spanish descent, kept as their mistresses free women of color, quadroons or octoroons, establishing second households for these second families in close proximity to their first. As offspring from these unions proliferated over time, a whole new ethnic segment of New Orleans society developed, a unified, proud, and secretive class who considered themselves superior to the black population of slaves and former slaves and, often, because of their plantation heritage in Santo Domingo, superior to the ruling white hierarchy as well. *Plaçage* was a system not only well known by the populace and officials but even condoned by the law; yet for outsiders, it remained a secret so closely guarded by locals that Cable's use of it in his stories and novels turned him into an outcast in the city of his birth. For Rice, whose subject matter always involves those who are, for whatever reason, excluded from the mainstream, these residents on the fringe of New Orleans society were understandably appealing as characters and symbols. Because Rice had access to material unavailable to Cable and spent years in research, her dramatization of that unique chapter in the city's history is to date the best imaginative re-creation of their remarkable history available in print.

4. Anne Rice, *Interview with the Vampire* (New York, 1976), 351.

Three of Valerie Martin's novels with New Orleans settings, *Set in Motion, Alexandra,* and *A Recent Martyr,* and several short stories in *The Consolation of Nature* derive their Gothicism, as does the work of William Faulkner and Eudora Welty, from the peculiar nature of the locale and the characters rather than from the supernatural. In one story, "Death Goes to a Party," however, the real and the surreal blend seamlessly, and in the novel *The Great Divorce,* Martin moves beyond the realm of the actual to relate the tale of a legendary nineteenth-century "Cat Woman" of Louisiana, who is paralleled and contrasted to the two modern protagonists.

Martin's view of New Orleans is epitomized in a memorable and paradoxical passage that concludes *A Recent Martyr,* in which she describes the city as both a physical and psychological island, connected "only by our own endeavor" to the mainland United States: "The river from which we drink drains a continent; it has to be purified for days before we can stomach it. We smile to ourselves when people from more fashionable centers find us provincial, for if we are free of one thing, it's fashion. The future holds a simple promise. We are well below sea level, and inundation is inevitable. We are content, for now, to have our heads above water."[5] Her perception that New Orleans is a city unavoidably controlled by its atmosphere and by the isolation imposed by geography, which has prevented its becoming a modern southern metropolis like Atlanta or Houston, is central to her narrative approach.

This insular and insulated, backwater and water-bound condition serves as crucial background for much of Martin's fiction and, on occasion, instills in her characters a claustrophobic terror as well as persistent thoughts of possible inundation. One character in *The Great Divorce* observes that "everything was too close together . . . beauty to ugliness, death to life."[6] In "The Consolation of Nature," a short story in the collection of the same name, the mother, listening to the torrentially insistent rain that has beaten down the trees and shrubbery and driven rats from the sewers and into homes and other buildings, imagines the Mississippi River, "swollen with brown water, swirling along hurriedly toward the Gulf of Mexico."[7] Characters in both *A Recent Martyr* and *The Great Divorce* descend the levee at Jackson Square to the Mississippi

---

5. Valerie Martin, *A Recent Martyr* (Boston, 1987), 204.
6. Valerie Martin, *The Great Divorce* (New York, 1994), 295.
7. Valerie Martin, *The Consolation of Nature* (Boston, 1988), 1.

River, where they encounter hordes of rats, a ubiquitous and unavoidable pest in a peninsular city in the Deep South. The river, one character in *The Great Divorce* observes, "was so polluted that it was a kind of anti-water, not useful for cleaning anything" (296).

The very atmosphere of New Orleans and its environs, decayed and polluted, seems to inspire paranoia in Martin's characters, as though fear emanates from the sidewalks and old walls and especially from the lush and uncontrollable vegetation. In *Alexandra*, Mona tells Claude that she has dreamed of him "lying in the street and some Negroes had cut off your hands."[8] Even the St. Charles streetcar becomes, as Claude watches it, somehow menacing, "lurching around the corner at Carrollton, hurtling toward us in the darkness, bereft of passengers" (58). Walking along Bourbon Street, Camille, in *The Great Divorce,* is inexplicably frightened by the pervasive sense of carnality as, passing by strip shows and clubs, she sees in glass cases photos of sex acts being performed. For her, this environment constitutes "a world she knew nothing about, a kind of tear in the fabric of life through which she could discern unfathomable depths, a strange, lewd, black abyss into which anyone who wasn't careful might fall," and where were paired "men and women, women and women, or women who had been men or were still partly men" (216). A similar kind of terror grips the protagonist in John Rechy's 1963 novel *City of Night,* when his strange "pilgrimage" around the country ends at carnival time in New Orleans, and he senses in that "casbah world" a "Biblical feeling of Doom—of the city soon to be destroyed, razed, toppled."[9]

Martin employs in her narratives some of the unique New Orleans customs that add an air of mystery to the city, for example, the above-ground burials in European-style cemeteries, their stark white tombs in seemingly endless rows that often startle outsiders with their persistent evocations of mortality. In *The Great Divorce,* Ellen, driving to work in the early morning, notes that "there was still a fog over the monuments in the graveyard, so that the angels and animals seemed to be materializing from the mist" (337). Masking, a favorite pastime in the City That Care Forgot, especially during the long Carnival season, is crucial to the plot of "Death Goes to a Party," in *The Consolation of Nature.* As Atala, the protagonist, dressed as Death, moves among other party guests wear-

8. Valerie Martin, *Alexandra* (New York, 1979), 37.
9. John Rechy, *City of Night* (New York, 1963), 308.

ing bizarre costumes, including those of a gorilla, a nun, and a wolfman, she realizes that "no one would recognize her, yet no one would fail to recognize her. She was that dreadful figure we have all seen in pictures, in our dreams, in brooding visions, in moments of danger" (62). Death seems ever present in New Orleans, given the prevalence of violent crime, the dangerously high levels of harmful chemicals in the water and air, the widespread poverty, and the cemeteries that intrude on the senses, all aspects of the city that are reflected in Martin's work. In *The Great Divorce,* Camille enters the French Quarter late at night, where she feels herself falling into an unknown and terrifying space, hears creatures stirring in the narrow, dark streets, "cool, damp, and sinister," and realizes that "this was their time, rats and waterbugs, a few cats . . . and the sleepless restless humans who like Camille dreaded the coming of daylight" (291–92). In the dark Decatur street bar she enters, the customers are "dangerous and desperate" and have "good cause to avoid light" (299).

Despite the foreboding aspect of the city, Martin, like the other authors under consideration, is drawn to the beauty of the place, as in *A Recent Martyr,* in which the French Quarter is described as the best place to be during the plague: walking there, one heard "the pleasant sound of the water beating resolutely against concrete, against glass, everywhere with the same gentle insistence." In such an atmosphere, the "senses expanded, odors arrived at the nose in a liquid rush, sounds were filtered by heavy air, eyes that had been crossed from squinting at the light slowly cleared and rested on a scene softened through a mist" (101). Finally, the contradictory nature of the composition of New Orleans supplies Martin, as well as the other writers, with much of the inspiration for her work.

Martin's vision of the city derives power from her effective evocation of the characteristic atmosphere of the various neighborhoods and her empathy for the local character, tinged with superstition, motivated by an ingrained devotion to Roman Catholicism admixed with voodoo and other folk religions. In one of the three entwined plots of *The Great Divorce,* she relates the story of Elizabeth, a young nineteenth-century Creole woman who marries an outsider, a German immigrant named Hermann Schlaeger. The conflict of the story as well as its ultimate tragedy emanates from the contrast and even animosity between the two cultures. Paul, a twentieth-century New Orleanian who is writing a book about Elizabeth and her husband, thinks that perhaps Schlaeger had

Valerie Martin, creator of Gothic novels with a New Orleans
setting and atmosphere
Photo by W. Kenneth Holditch

married a Creole hoping to gain a position for himself among the plantation aristocracy, an attempt doomed to failure because "Creole society
was inbred to the point of genetic exhaustion and determined to remain
so" (6). No matter how rich he might be, the outsider would always find
the doors of the French Quarter or plantation homes closed to him, and
even in death, he would be denied burial in St. Louis Cemetery. The Creoles consider Schlaeger a barbarian, and in turn he deems them weak,
shiftless, overly fond of dancing and indulgence of the flesh, "contempt-
ible in manners, language, but particularly in efficiency" (30), the last being a charge frequently brought against the Creoles by outsiders, Ameri-

146

can and foreign, since the founding of the Louisiana colony. The same judgment, indeed in much the same language, is to be found in the letters sent to Washington in the early 1800s by the first American governor of the newly acquired colony, W. C. C. Claiborne, and in the fiction and nonfiction of George Washington Cable.

One local element that weaves a strong and colorful Gothic thread into Martin's narrative pattern as into that of Anne Rice involves the *griffes*, free people of mixed blood living in a twilight zone between white Creoles on the one hand and slaves on the other, a world in which voodoo and other exotic practices are commonplace. The strange relationship between the various strata of the races in Louisiana puzzles the German, who thinks of the *griffes*, the products of *plaçage*, as "creatures of the city," most of whom do not speak English. The sons of the alliances between white men and women of color might study art or furniture-making in Paris and then, "arrogant and difficult," return to New Orleans, where even the quadroons will not marry them (93). Among this group (many with family ties to the island of Hispaniola), voodoo flourishes, and Hermann is appalled not only by his wife's Catholicism but also by her belief in "evil spirits and the magical powers of powders made from roots" (30) and her dependence on a hairdresser-adviser, a character reminiscent of the famous voodoo queen Marie Laveau. In another of the three plots in *The Great Divorce*, Ellen listens to a popular recording of an ersatz voodoo chant and thinks that those who attempt to "summon the spirits of animals to set them free" believe themselves not to be animals, and thus "the great divorce" between humanity and nature "had already begun" (337).

Despite similarities in their uses of the grotesque, there are major differences between the narrative methods of Anne Rice and Valerie Martin. Their approaches to development of character are diametrically opposed: Martin takes seemingly ordinary people who may, on first encounter, appear to be of little interest, and gradually peels away the outer layers to reveal surprising, sometimes appealing, sometimes appalling qualities beneath, whereas Rice creates extraordinary characters (vampires, *gens de couleur*, and witches) and makes them appear credible, even ordinary, in their function as metaphors for the outsider in society. For Rice, the use of what she calls the "comic book character with fangs and wearing a cape" allows her to recapture "what had been everyday reality in New Orleans for me growing up." Martin's characters, on the other hand, are haunted by deeply ingrained, even atavistic fears that become actualized: the dead rats on the riverbank near Jackson Square, the enormous roaches and other insects that infest the city, a severed head. While Martin's language is understated and controlled, Rice's style is more reminiscent of nineteenth-century romanticism, "directly influenced by New Orleans," she says, and "not just by the colors, the textures, the beauty" of the place. Commenting on accusations that hers is an "overblown and humid style," she insists that this "could be a description of New Orleans itself."

It is, finally, the setting against which characters are placed that differentiates the New Orleans aspect of the two authors' works. For Valerie Martin, the traditional fear associated with Gothicism often emanates from the open spaces of the city. She casts grotesque scenes, for example, in Jackson Square, in Père Antoine Alley beside the cathedral, on the banks of the Mississippi, on streetcars. Rice, on the other hand, although she uses cemeteries and the streets at night for her scenes, is more likely to employ interiors: a townhouse on St. Louis or Royal Street, the cathedral, the old French Opera House, a ruined uptown mansion.

Both authors have frequently and openly expressed admiration and love for their hometown, no matter the degree to which they portray its more unappetizing elements. Rice, shortly after her return to "the landscape of my childhood" to live, found that "the city is as beautiful as I ever remembered it to be. . . . You know, there was always that tremendous almost painful longing for what was lost." As a result, she states, she could have returned to find that her city did not match up to her dream of it, but New Orleans "is such an intense place wherever you go that I don't think memory can enhance it." Once she had returned, she says, she was again able to relish the "other-worldly quality of this city," to write "with the sound of the rain falling on the banana trees, the smell of the river breeze coming in the window," and to relish at twilight "the golden moment when the sky is shot with red and purple and gold."

Valerie Martin identifies a passage in her novel *A Recent Martyr* as the best expression of her feelings for the city.[10] The protagonist, Emma Miller, having returned to New Orleans after several days' absence, ponders the distinctly grotesque elements of the place and wonders why she

10. The observations of Valerie Martin included in this essay are taken from conversations between her and the author over the past three decades.

has come back to live in an atmosphere of "decay, of vicious, florid, natural cycles," of "hateful, humid, murderously hot afternoons," but she knows that she will be unable to live anywhere "but in this swamp." She admits to being enchanted by chameleons, moss on the sides of trees, plaintain palms, and the scum on the bayous, and the "colorful conversation of the lazy, suspicious, pleasure-loving populace" (204).

For both Rice and Martin, the allure of the city is paradoxical—there is decay amid the beauty—and through use of the Gothic they effect a remarkable synthesis of the two aspects. Much of the success of their New Orleans novels comes from their clear perception of the contradictory elements that make up what is perhaps the most unusual city in the United States.

Oddly enough, the mystery novel did not become a staple of New Orleans literature until recent years. In the 1930s and 1940s, two local authors attempted to adapt the city to the genre, with only limited success. The popular historical novelist Gwen Bristow and her husband, Bruce Manning, collaborated on *The Mardi Gras Murders,* focusing on a New Orleans phenomenon that would seem to be a natural for a mystery, but the work is second rate. John Dickson Carr's *Papa Là-Bas* suffers from the usual problems of books written by the tourist: the author concentrates on the distinctive elements and stories of the city—the Lalaurie haunted house, Marie Laveau and voodoo, and Judah P. Benjamin—producing a mishmash of inaccurate history and myth.[11]

In recent years, however, a promising new generation of mystery writers has emerged, among them Julie Smith, James Lee Burke, and Chris Wiltz, three authors whose works represent well the positive direction in which the genre has been taken in the city. What combination of circumstances may have led to this sudden abundance of "tales of ratiocination" it is impossible to tell, but more and more practitioners of the genre have appeared, each with a unique approach. Many of them have produced fiction that is effective precisely because they create plots and characters that emanate from the environment of New Orleans, rather than choosing the city as a setting because of its exotic and romantic nature.

Even when Julie Smith was not a full-time resident, she retained close

11. Gwen Bristow, *The Mardi Gras Murders* (New York, 1932); John Dickson Carr, *Papa Là-Bas* (New York, 1968).

ties with New Orleans, which continues to provide inspiration for her writing and to serve as the setting for her best novels. The extent to which the city is an integral part of her fiction is indicated by her titles: *New Orleans Mourning, The Axeman's Blues, Jazz Funeral, New Orleans Beat,* and *The House of Blues.* Her detective, Skip Langdon, is, in many ways, a typical "uptown girl," christened at Trinity Episcopal Church, educated at Louise McGeehee School and at Newcomb College, where she belonged to the right sorority. She has, however, openly rebelled against that stereotypical upbringing, first by flunking out of college, then by eschewing the role of Carnival queen or maid and the socially appropriate marriage. Finally, she chooses the life of a policewoman in the French Quarter rather than that of the proper Garden District matron who rules over husband, children, and servants, plays bridge, belongs to "literary" clubs and the Junior League, works with the appropriate charities, and lunches at Commander's Palace with women from her own social stratum. The drastic turnabout in character and style of life, exemplified by Skip's involvement with the two disparate urban districts, uptown and downtown, are skillfully portrayed in *New Orleans Mourning,* in which she has not yet broken away from her background, and in the succeeding works, as she becomes more and more independent of the influences that shape the lives of her parents, her brother, and many of her uptown contemporaries.

Smith's narratives cover three decades of New Orleans history, from the 1960s to the present, with repeated references to specific neighborhoods and streets, a wide variety of well-known local restaurants (Casamento's, the Clover Grill, the Rib Room), bars (the Napoleon House and the Dream Palace), grocery stores (Schwegmann's), and recognizable New Orleans characters. She describes in *The Axeman's Blues* this "weird town" as being "rife with types, losers, and weirdos,"[12] for example, two described in *New Orleans Beat:* the "aging Deke," identified by Smith as "a very specific New Orleans type" (79), and a man who is "vaguely handsome in that clean-cut fraternity boy way so many New Orleans men were blessed with" (97). *Jazz Funeral* opens with a brief characterization of the city, employing three axioms many residents will immediately recognize: "The newcomer is told three things by the old

12. Julie Smith, *The Axeman's Blues* (New York, 1991), 4, 16.

Julie Smith, writer of detective fiction featuring Skip Langdon, an "uptown girl" who has rebelled against her upbringing
Photo © David G. Spielman, 1994

New Orleans hand: don't walk on the lake side of the Quarter, don't drink the water, and always take a United Cab."[13]

Through Skip Langdon, Smith comments on distinctive elements of New Orleans: its small-town quality, its rigidly structured social order, its hedonistic lifestyle, and its division into discrete neighborhoods, particularly uptown and downtown, different as though separated by thousands of miles, a dichotomy that has fed the creative imaginations of such widely diverse authors as George Washington Cable and John Kennedy Toole. Skip Langdon's portrayals of other districts, such as Lakeview, which she

13. Julie Smith, *Jazz Funeral* (New York, 1993), 3.

terms "Ozzie-and-Harriet land" (108) in *The Axeman's Blues,* represent a precise reading by the author of the attitudes of many New Orleanians. Smith acknowledges some flaws in the city's environment and character: for example, uptown society, including the powerful segment that controls the clubs, Carnival, and much of the city's business, is a closed one, excluding those who were not born there or who lack the appropriate class background, a tightly knit unit that, Skip acknowledges, can "shun you or embrace you" and even "destroy you financially" (1).

In several novels, Smith compares San Francisco to New Orleans, contrasting the health-conscious attitudes and accelerated pace of the former to the slow, even torpid, sensual, and luxurious lifestyle of the latter. Alex in *Axeman's Blues,* a disgruntled native who is back home after having lived for years in California, exaggerates the negative qualities when he asserts that New Orleans has nothing but "falling-down buildings, cholesterol instead of food, and brimstone instead of weather" (124). Skip acknowledges its hedonistic excesses when she states that "New Orleans could wreck your liver and poison your blood." She asserts, however, that despite its murderous summer heat ("in August it could break your spirit"), New Orleans could "teach you tricks of the heart you thought Tennessee Williams was just kidding about" (1). The ghost of the playwright, which haunts the city and its literature in a positive way, is often evidenced in Smith's writing, as in *New Orleans Beat,* where Skip thinks, *"Well, what the hell, depending on the kindness of strangers made this city famous"* (184). Such passages, blending as they do the real New Orleans with that vividly imagined by its great writers, exemplify the degree to which Julie Smith has been able to distill, refine, and encapsulate the city's essence.

The New Orleans of James Lee Burke and Chris Wiltz's novels is a dark and often sleazy underworld of psychotic dope dealers, sadistic mobsters, and disillusioned, sometimes corrupt or easily corruptible policemen. Whereas Julie Smith's detective is a former debutante from uptown and her plots center on the actions of middle- and upper-class characters, Burke's detective is a Cajun, and Wiltz's is an idealistic ex-policeman from the Irish Channel; their adventures involve a wide range of types, many from that large fringe element in the city who live outside the law, in reality as in fiction.

Like Anne Rice and Valerie Martin, James Lee Burke perceives and employs the paradoxical elements of the city—the good and the bad, the

James Lee Burke, creator of a fictional series featuring a Cajun detective,
Dave Robicheaux
Photo © Tomm Furch, 1995

appealing and the disgusting, the beautiful and the corrupt. That he is
not a native of the city, although he is a Louisianian, has not prevented
his becoming one of the keenest observers and recorders of its distinctive
and multifaceted pattern of neighborhoods, ethnic groups, and classes.
The city often serves as a setting for the action of his novels, much of it
centered on Mafia activity and the corrupt enterprises of both major and
petty criminals, who, as he describes them, hold "the franchise on the
worm's-eye view of the world" and are "joyless, indifferent to specula-
tions about mortality."[14]

14. James Lee Burke, *In the Electric Mist with Confederate Dead* (New York, 1993),
101.

It is worth noting that New Orleans was the birthplace of the American mafia, which had its origins along the riverfront and Decatur Street in the late nineteenth century, and no one has a better understanding than Burke of the presence and effect of organized crime and the levels of corruption that reach deep into the city's history and culture and day-to-day life. Without resorting to stereotypes, he creates mob leaders and their flunkies who exemplify the local breed, with the ethnic animosities that have existed between the Irish and the Sicilians since late in the last century, their mutual contempt for blacks, and their Catholic piety, in ironic juxtaposition to their viciousness.

Burke knows well that much of the attraction of the city for outsiders derives from its corruption, its reputation as Sin City, where the Iowa Rotarian and the mortician from Michigan can forget their compunctions for a night or a week, as observed in a humorous passage from *In the Electric Mist with Confederate Dead:* "Without its pagan and decadent ambience, its strip shows, hookers, burlesque spielers, taxi pimps, and brain-damaged street dopers, the city would be as attractive to most tourists as an agrarian theme park in western Nebraska" (101). Burke's detective Dave Robicheaux perceives that there are "two populations" and "almost two sensory climates" in the French Quarter: there is the Vieux Carré of residents and tourists on the one hand and, on the other, the city of night in which college students, soldiers, sailors, and other visitors from the United States and abroad move among the "grifters, Murphy artists, dips and stalls, coke and shag dealers," prostitutes, strippers, and others who "view ordinary human beings as carnival workers do rubes; they look upon their victims with contempt, sometimes with loathing" (101).

Yet Robicheaux, possessed of a sensitive and perceptive consciousness, is always alert to the beauty to be found, sometimes in the midst of corruption. Often in the novel, lyrical descriptions of the almost painful beauty of the city are sharply juxtaposed to the narration of violent events and gross circumstances, which are, unfortunately, as much a part of the real New Orleans as of the one Burke has imagined. In *Dixie City Jam*, Robicheaux observes as he drives along St. Charles Avenue the "gray mist through which the old iron, green-painted streetcars would make their way along the tracks like emissaries from the year 1910."[15]

---

15. James Lee Burke, *Dixie City Jam* (New York, 1994), 8.

The French Quarter he considers to be at its best in the morning, permeated by the aromas of "coffee and fresh-baked bread in the small grocery stores," and balconies "overgrown with a tangle of potted roses, bougainvillea, azaleas, and flaming hibiscus," a place where everything is "so perfect that you felt you had stepped inside an Utrillo painting" (15). Almost immediately, however, he becomes aware of yet "another reality," of "the smell of urine in doorways, left nightly by the homeless and the psychotic, and the broken fragments of tiny ten-dollar cocaine vials that glinted in the gutters like rats' teeth" (15). His vision of the city includes not only the Quarter but other, even sleazier environments, for example, the long stretch of Airline Highway possessed of "that quasi-rural culture that always characterized the peckerwood South" (*In the Electric Mist with Confederate Dead*, 107–108).

Despite a few minor flaws (a tendency, for example, to make factual errors—troublesome to New Orleanians, who, given as they generally are to spinning imaginative myths about their city, are nevertheless quick to spot a mistake about locale or food), Burke, with his distinctive and perceptive view of the city at its best and worst, and his paradoxical blend of tough portrayals of the sordid aspects with what might almost constitute paeans of praise for local charms and beauty, has established for himself a unique position among the city's chroniclers in fiction.

The New Orleans of Chris Wiltz's novels is a backwash of modern civilization, an easygoing, often corrupt place in which life, as she observes in *The Emerald Lizard*, is "so slow and lazy that things caught on several years after leaving the rest of the country."[16] Like Valerie Martin, she perceives and portrays the claustrophobic nature of the city, a result of its topography as well as the closeness of family ties. It is a "deceptive" place, her detective asserts, like Lake Pontchartrain, which hides deep beneath the surface of its waters "all kinds of pollution."[17] Like Burke, she takes her readers into urban areas generally unknown to any but natives or long-time residents. Her settings are as varied as a pool hall in the Irish Channel; a bar on Arabella Street; Veterans' Highway and its prefabricated buildings and shopping malls with western or other ersatz motifs, an area in which, as Wiltz's detective, Neal Rafferty, observes in *The Emerald Lizard*, "the view isn't particularly scenic unless you happen to like

---

16. Chris Wiltz, *The Emerald Lizard* (New York, 1991), 29.
17. Chris Wiltz, *The Killing Circle* (New York, 1981), 115.

Chris Wiltz, whose detective stories reflect the claustrophobic
nature of New Orleans
Photo © David G. Spielman, 1995

a lot of neon" (139); and a neighborhood on the West Bank called West-wego, of which one of its inhabitants observes that it "might as well be in China, huh?" (3). As in other New Orleans neighborhoods, closed to out-siders, residents there live in "their own little world," and Rafferty, "a good New Orleans boy," freely admits his "prejudice against the West Bank" (25), a typical reaction to neighborhoods across the river. With an astounding degree of *sangfroid,* equal to that of James Lee Burke, Wiltz portrays the multiple layers of low life from the top to the bottom of the social scale.

Acutely conscious of the sharply drawn social lines in the city, Rafferty tells us in *The Emerald Lizard* that he was born "on the wrong side of the tracks" in a camelback double in the Irish Channel, "too far away from

St. Charles Avenue" (56). Like the characters of Julie Smith and others, he acknowledges that uptown is a "closed society, open only to those who grew up there or were accepted by tacit agreement" (54), a statement that many of those who know the city will freely endorse as fact. Interestingly, these sharply drawn social barriers do not, however, prevent close friendships between residents of different neighborhoods and strata of the population. Neal and his friend Maurice are, he states, as "different as the parts of town we come from," a difference he attributes to the fact that Maurice is from the "cool and shady Garden District," a tree-lined area in which the "money, the mansions, and the gentility" are to be found, whereas in Neal's neighborhood, the houses are "separated by alleyways and the people are tough" (9). Although the proper "up-towner" belongs to the Krewe of Comus, the Boston Club, and the Lawn Tennis Club, "all of which meant he was as blue-blooded a New Orleanian as you can be," Neal rather proudly asserts that he does not generally attend Mardi Gras balls or fund-raising parties (55–56). As he moves through the contrasting neighborhoods, he, like Dave Robicheaux, is acutely sensitive to both the corruption lurking beneath the façades of everyday life and the beauty that is abundantly evident. The French Quarter at night, for example, is a "lunatic asylum" populated by dangerous drivers and drunken revelers, by panhandlers "looking for a handout for their next high, for condoms, or for their religious organizations" amid a cacophony of unpleasant sounds in dark side streets "safe only for junkies or pimps." But in the morning, when "dawn has tipped the rooftops with translucent color and the dampness smells like freshly ground parsley," Neal's chest tightens "with a quiet thoughtful kind of pleasure," he tells us in *The Killing Circle* (39–40). Like most of the characters in most of the books I discuss here, Neal Rafferty is a chauvinist when it comes to his own New Orleans.

The works of Burke, Smith, and Wiltz demonstrate that the detective novel, like fiction in the Gothic mode, is remarkably suited to New Orleans. The atmosphere of the city, its history, its ancient buildings, and the well-known corruption that plagues law enforcement agencies and other branches of government provide fertile ground in which the mystery writer can work. These authors have made effective use of an abundant supply of local material to produce novels that are a distinctive part of the city's literary tradition.

Ellen Gilchrist, a native of Mississippi but with family connections in

New Orleans, understands the social complexity of life among the upper classes of the city so well that publication of her first work of fiction, *In the Land of Dreamy Dreams,* a collection of short stories that takes its title from the old song "Do You Know What It Means to Miss New Orleans," had members of uptown society scrambling to read it and find out if they had been "captured" by or "escaped" her wickedly ironic pen. She reads accurately the byzantine local social structure as a tightly restrictive club whose members rarely admit outsiders (that is, anyone arrived within the past century) into their august midst. That situation is effectively dramatized in "Rich," a short story in that first collection, in which Tom Wilson, Gilchrist's typical uptown aristocrat, spends most of his time, she writes, "gambling and hunting and fishing and being the life of the party at the endless round of dinners and cocktail parties and benefits and Mardi Gras functions that consume the lives of the Roman Catholic hierarchy that dominates the life of the city that care forgot."[18] Tom's wife, Letty, the perfect young uptown matron, had been Queen of Carnival in her debutante year and now proudly indulges in the privilege of flying the green, purple, and gold flag before her house every Carnival season as an acknowledgment of her superiority. Disturbed by the fact that their mentally defective adopted daughter is responsible for the accidental death of their own baby, Tom finally kills the girl, an "outsider" who has not found a place with them.

Like George Washington Cable before her, Gilchrist is not only a perceptive social commentator on the "Creoles," real and ersatz, but also a moral critic. In the title story of *In the Land of Dreamy Dreams,* LaGrande Magruder, daughter of an old, established uptown family and member of the Lawn Tennis Club, "the oldest and snottiest tennis club in the United States of America" (62), is willing to compromise her sense of honor and sportsmanship in a match with a new member, a Jewish woman from the North, a "Goddamned little new rich Yankee bitch" (60), as LaGrande terms her, all under the watchful eye (and approval) of the president of the organization. Lady Margaret Sarpie, an uptown resident from an old family in the story "Looking over Jordan," included in the National Book Award winner *Victory over Japan,* is appalled when she encounters at the Morning Call coffee shop an overly friendly couple, "the very worst of yankees who moved to New Orleans and started try-

---

18. Ellen Gilchrist, *In the Land of Dreamy Dreams* (Fayetteville, Ark., 1981), 8.

Ellen Gilchrist, a perceptive commentator on the New Orleans Creoles
and a moral critic of their ways
Photo by Pierre Walker III

ing to get right into everything. They had even bought an antebellum
house and restored it."[19] Clearly, they have intruded into what is for her a
"sacred" place, hallowed to her memory, for she recalls being taken as a
child by her father at night to the French Quarter to get a late newspaper
and "sit beside the levee dipping beignets into coffee," listening to fog-
horns on the Mississippi and the buzz of mosquitoes, while her father
conversed with friends and sometimes lifted her so she could watch the
New Orleans–style doughnuts being made in the kitchen. So sweet is the
memory that she thinks, "Plaisir . . . Joy to the world, sugar is come. . . .
It had made her family rich and her mother fat" (85–86). Now her father

19. Ellen Gilchrist, *Victory over Japan* (Boston, 1984), 84.

is dead and Morning Call has moved to Metairie, and Yankees are everywhere.

As these stories demonstrate, native New Orleanians tend to be by tradition *possessive* about their city, willing to share it for short periods but only if the outsider understands that he is merely there on a visit, no matter how extended, and has no vested rights in the sacred place or its customs. Paradoxically, however, residents of all the neighborhoods and from all levels of society are remarkably democratic in terms of many of their activities—sporting events, hunting, sexual liaisons, and even some social gatherings—a unique trait Gilchrist dramatizes in the short story from *In the Land of Dreamy Dreams* entitled "The Famous Poll at Jody's Bar." Jody's, the oldest tavern in the Irish Channel, did not welcome everyone wanting to drink, but "its regular customers included second- and third-generation drinkers from many walks of life. Descendants of Creole blue bloods mingled easily with house painters and delivery men stopping for a quick one on their route" (53). This cultural phenomenon is so common that she might be describing any number of old neighborhood bars around the city.

Gilchrist has a keen sense of the distinctive atmosphere of the city, perhaps sharpened by nostalgia (she has lived elsewhere for a number of years), and a talent for re-creating the sights, sounds, and smells familiar to residents. She knows well the "strange lassitude of New Orleans in summer" (*Victory over Japan*, 83), and in "The Lower Garden District Free Gravity Mule Blight or Rhoda, a Fable," the narrator observes that six P.M. "is the time of day in New Orleans when the light cools down, coming in at angles around the tombs in the cemeteries, between the branches of the live oak trees along the avenues, casting shadows across the yards, penetrating the glass of a million windows" (67). Traceleen, the wise and humorous black maid to an uptown family in one of the stories in *Victory over Japan*, wonders what nonresidents think when they see on television the heavy rains and flooding in New Orleans: "Because the thing the television can't show them is the smell. Not a bad smell, a cold clean smell like breathing in water. We're below the sea in south Louisiana and when the rains come we're in the sea" (255–56). Being below the sea, however, is acceptable for most New Orleanians, as both Valerie Martin and Ellen Gilchrist observe, if they can remain in the place dear to their hearts. Gilchrist, despite the satirical bent of her approach, clearly shares the affection for the city that is integral to all the writers discussed here.

No writer who has essayed the arduous and delicate task of portraying the intricacies of aristocratic uptown New Orleans has done so more successfully than Sheila Bosworth. Even Walker Percy, born in Alabama and reared in the Mississippi Delta, wrote as an outsider, looking at the complex family entanglements and the almost feudal relationships between wealthy whites and their black servants perceptively but without the finer distinctions one finds in Bosworth's narratives. Like John Kennedy Toole before her and her contemporary Ellen Gilchrist, Bosworth's view of this material is tinged with and illuminated by a keenly satiric sense of humor. An exemplary episode is the one in her second novel, *Slow Poison*, involving LaRue's Coiffure shop, whose "brutally candid beauticians" were hairdressers to Carnival queens and other ladies high in the New Orleans social sphere. After the salon closed and an abortion clinic opened in the building, elderly and unsuspecting matrons who appeared at the reception desk would be asked when they had last menstruated and try to remember, believing it to be part of some strange new treatment for the hair.[20]

In *Almost Innocent,* Bosworth's first novel, the protagonist, Clay-Lee Calvert, is a product of the environment in which she was born and has grown to maturity. During a troubled period of her life, she begins to sleep badly, "to awaken suddenly at sounds that had always been the background music of my life: the ghostly rattling of a streetcar somewhere on the avenue, the funereal piping of a boat whistle out on the Mississippi."[21] The characters in Bosworth's two novels move through the New Orleans atmosphere, aware of the ever-present threat of violence, accustomed to the debilitating heat and humidity but always conscious of it. Sis Honorine, the black woman who has cared for several generations of children of the family in *Almost Innocent,* is a font of folk wisdom and philosophy, such as her observation "that New Orleans damp could chill anybody's soul after a while" (232). When the family returns to live across the lake, she thanks God that they are in Covington: "No more mean wolves walkin' the streets instead of human people, like in

20. Sheila Bosworth, *Slow Poison* (New York, 1992).
21. Sheila Bosworth, *Almost Innocent* (New York, 1984), 177.

New Orleans. You can't open your door without letting in ax murderers" (234).

What perhaps most distinguishes Bosworth's insight into the New Orleans social establishment is the innate though unassuming authority with which she speaks. She knows from experience the customs, mores, and prejudices of the uptowners, especially those who are Roman Catholic. Other writers may well be and, indeed, are perceptive observers and recorders of the peculiarities of the New Orleans elite, but Bosworth is a reporter not only of what she has been taught and has observed but also of what she has personally experienced. With an insight unavailable to the researcher, she speaks about ethnic animosities in the city, the odd habits of socialites, the time-honored practices of Carnival, the occasional tyranny of nuns and priests. Only in New Orleans (a phrase, by the way, much loved and employed by natives) could many of the scenes in her novels (or for that matter, those of the other writers discussed here) occur. There is, for example, a humorous—and for the local reader, a perhaps scandalous—scene in which Uncle Baby brings an octoroon woman to a Mardi Gras party in a family apartment of the Upper Pontalba, or there is the proprietarial way in which natives create their own "traditions," such as the "white lunch" at Antoine's that two of the men of the family have made an annual event (136).

Merrill Shackleford, at once a wonderful exemplar of a particular New Orleans type and a well-limned character in his own right, is described in *Slow Poison* as the son of a former Queen of Carnival and member of the decayed gentry prevalent above Louisiana Avenue; he is poor but well established and accepted, living in ancient houses with bad wiring, bed linens for drapes, and black maids "serving Vienna sausage on heirloom silver trays to the ladies of the house." This privileged if penurious upbringing does not prevent his knowing well the "caprices of his native city's ruling class," and Bosworth, in one amusing but telling aside, remarks that he "did not make the mistake of instantly assuming that a New Orleans girl named Aimee Desiree was a whore just because of the name" (39). Tucked neatly into her narrative fabric are to be found many such clever observations on local mores, so low key as to be easily overlooked, for example, one character's remark in *Slow Poison* that New Orleanians "hadn't been scared of anything since Reconstruction, except that it might rain on Mardi Gras" (176).

No one since Grace King has painted a more loving portrait of the city than Bosworth does with subtle but identifiable detail, although she, like the other authors under consideration, is fully cognizant of its faults. This ambivalent response to the place of her birth and rearing—one is reminded of Quentin Compson's assertion about the South in *Absalom, Absalom!:* "I dont hate it! I dont hate it!"[22]—is often evident in the novels of Bosworth. Shackleford calls Louisiana "the state of exaggeration," insisting that "the men are too passionate, the food is too rich, the women are too beautiful," to which Eamon adds that "the climate's a pain in the ass, too" (278). *Slow Poison* contains a concise summation of the paradoxical nature of Louisiana: rumored to be "the end of the earth," it nevertheless has, along with its "humid crevices where the swamp rats breed and thrive," a "tragic reputation" and "sweet old places," and for the "Southerner, sweet and sad mean the same thing." It is a state, separated from the rest of the country, which "could kill you if you sat still and let it" (27). Although many of the New Orleans authors from the past two centuries have expressed similar feelings, none of them, it seems to me, reach quite the intensity demonstrated by Bosworth in these passages.

Each of the authors discussed in this essay is distinctive in his or her own way, sharing as they do the bountiful material afforded them by New Orleans and an obvious passion for what they write about. Common threads in all their fiction include observations about various aspects of the place—its provincialism, the discrete and disparate neighborhoods, the sharply defined social structure—and of its people—their peculiarities, the strong criminal element, and the existence of corruption in one form or another, a distinctly New Orleans corruption, in all levels of government and business. That New Orleans, a large sprawling city, has retained many qualities of a small town is often reiterated in these authors' novels, for example, in *The Killing Circle,* when Chris Wiltz's detective encounters an old schoolmate and enemy from Redemptorist High School and thinks, "This damn town is entirely too small" (65), and in *The Emerald Lizard,* he thinks, "sometimes it seems not more than a couple of hundred people live there and they all seem to be related" (95). In *New Orleans Beat,* Julie Smith's Skip Langdon marvels at the villagelike quality of the city, thinking sometimes that "it was only tiny if you stayed within certain class and racial boundaries, but she was always being

22. William Faulkner, *Absalom, Absalom!* (New York, 1936), 378.

proved wrong," rediscovering that it was a city in which "you talked to whom you knew, and you just about always knew someone" (63).

New Orleans is a city famous for the indulgence of the senses, and the fiction of its contemporary authors reflects and comments on the generally hedonistic, sensuous, and sensual nature of the populace. There are repeated references to the easygoing attitude toward sexuality; to the passion for food and drink among the residents; to restaurants and their chefs, waiters, and recipes; and to bars and various drinks, such as the Sazerac, a New Orleans creation. Characters in Bosworth's novels dine at Galatoire's and Antoine's, drink Old Fashioneds and Royal beer, and smoke Picayune cigarettes, a favorite local brand. Burke's characters are more likely to be found at the Pearl Oyster Bar on St. Charles or at Mandina's in Mid City, while Julie Smith's detective drinks with her French Quarter friends at the Napoleon House, eats at Casamento's, and, on mandatory reunions with her uptown family, at Commander's Palace. At Dante's by the River, two characters in Gilchrist's *Victory over Japan* dine in typical New Orleans fashion on "Crab Thibodeaux and Shrimp Mousse and Softshell Crabs Richard" and roast quail prepared from "a recipe with a secret sauce perfected in Drew, Mississippi" (68). Although such details might seem extraneous in fiction set in other cities, in a New Orleans novel, they are essential elements identifying the characters.

Clearly, the muse of literature is still alive and well in New Orleans, no matter what her current avatar may be—casquette girl, voodienne, Queen of Comus, Storyville madame, or that aging courtesan shunning the sunlight imagined by Faulkner in *New Orleans Sketches*. Although I am writing here only about those authors whose work focuses specifically on New Orleans, I should point out one interesting phenomenon of the local literary scene: there have always been authors who chose for one reason or another to live there but not necessarily to write about the city to any great extent, among them Walt Whitman in the 1840s and Sherwood Anderson in the 1920s. Currently, Richard Ford, one of the best contemporary American novelists, resides in the city, but none of his works have been set there, and in his fiction he refers to New Orleans only in passing references, sometimes transposing names of local streets and businesses to other cities.

An abundance of writers, then, still share Walker Percy's devotion to the city that he expressed in the title of an essay, "New Orleans, Mon Amour." The seven authors and their works discussed above demonstrate that creativity flourishes in all the disparate neighborhoods, even though enclaves of writers no longer gather in cramped rooms and apartments on the narrow old streets and alleyways of the French Quarter to offer one another communal support and comfort. What Cleanth Brooks very aptly remarked about the city twenty years ago is still appropriate: "New Orleans has become one of the cities of the mind, and is therefore immortal." It is, of course, the authors who have written of it with devotion and power who have exalted it to that ideal realm.

Valerie Martin with W. Kenneth Holditch in the courtyard of the Maison de Ville in New Orleans
Photo by Patrick Van Hoorbeek

Contributors

THOMAS BONNER, JR., professor of English at Xavier University of Louisiana, is a native of New Orleans. His M.A. (1968) and Ph.D. (1975) in English are from Tulane University. In 1991–92, he was Distinguished Visiting Professor at the United States Air Force Academy. Currently, he holds a Henry C. McBay Research Fellowship to study John Faulkner, his writing, and his art. During 1982–83, he received an Andrew W. Mellon postdoctoral fellowship. He has written *The Kate Chopin Companion* (1988) and *William Faulkner: The William B. Wisdom Collection* (1980) and has edited *Above Ground: Stories About Life and Death by New Southern Writers* (1993) and *Immortelles: Poems of Life and Death by New Southern Writers* (1995). Since 1982 he has edited the *Xavier Review*. His essays have appeared in books, among them *The History of Southern Literature,* and in journals, such as the *Southern Quarterly* and *Resources for American Literary Study.* In 1980 he directed "Moonlight and Malaise: Literary New Orleans," a lecture series sponsored by the New Orleans Public Library and the National Endowment for the Humanities.

VIOLET HARRINGTON BRYAN, associate professor of English at Xavier University of Louisiana, was educated at Mount Holyoke College (B.A., 1970) and Harvard University (M.A., 1972; Ph.D., 1981). She is the author of *The Myth of New Orleans in Literature: A Dialogue of Race and Gender* (1993) and a contributor to *Louisiana Women Writers,* ed-

ited by Dorothy Brown and Barbara Ewell, and to two specialized ency-
clopedias—*Black Women: A Historical Encyclopedia*, edited by Darlene
Clark Hine, and *Notable Black American Women*, edited by Jessie Carney Smith. A specialist in American and African American literature, she
has published articles in various journals, such as the *CLA Journal*, the
Mississippi Quarterly, and *Sage*.

DAVID C. ESTES teaches southern literature and folklore at Loyola University in New Orleans. He has edited books on two Louisiana writers,
Thomas Bangs Thorpe and Ernest J. Gaines. He shares Zora Neale Hurston's ethnographic interest in African American folk religion in New
Orleans and has documented the rituals and preaching traditions of female ministers in the Spiritual churches there.

W. KENNETH HOLDITCH, research professor of English at the University of New Orleans, was educated at Southwestern University at Mem-
phis (B.A., 1955) and the University of Mississippi (M.A., 1957; Ph.D.,
1961). He is the founding publisher and editor of the *Tennessee Williams
Journal* and has published short stories, poems, and essays on Faulkner,
Williams, Lillian Hellman, and other southern writers. He has created
and conducts literary tours of New Orleans.

INEZ HOLLANDER LAKE, adjunct professor of English, Metropolitan
State College of Denver, was born in Velsen, The Netherlands. She was
educated at Leiden University, The Netherlands (B.A., 1989), the University of Leicester, Great Britain (M.A., 1989), and the Catholic University
of Nijmegen, The Netherlands (Ph.D., 1995). Her book *Reluctant Southerner: The Life and Work of Hamilton Basso* will be published in 1998 by
Louisiana State University Press.

THOMAS J. RICHARDSON is professor of English and coordinator of
senior honors at the University of Southern Mississippi, where he has
taught since 1971. He was chair of the Department of English from 1983
to 1988. He studied at the University of Southern Mississippi (B.A.,
1962), the University of Alabama (M.A., 1965), and Vanderbilt University (Ph.D., 1975). His teaching and research interests are in American
and southern literature, and his work includes *"The Grandissimes":
Centennial Essays* (1981) as well as essays on Cable, Twain, Tennessee

Williams, Will Percy, William Styron, and Larry Brown, among others. He has written on Louisiana literature in *The History of Southern Literature* (1985) and *The Encyclopedia of Southern Culture* (1989).

WALTER B. RIDEOUT is Harry Hayden Clark Professor of English Emeritus at the University of Wisconsin at Madison, where he served as chair of the English Department from 1965 to 1968. He was educated at Colby College (B.A.) and Harvard University (M.A. and Ph.D.). From 1949 to 1962 he taught at Northwestern University. In 1951–52 he shared a Newberry Library fellowship with Howard Mumford Jones, and in 1958–59, he held a Guggenheim fellowship. He is the author of *The Radical Novel in the United States* (1956); editor of *The Experience of Prose* (1960), *Caesar's Column*, by Ignatius Donnelly (1960), and *Sherwood Anderson: A Collection of Critical Essays* (1974); and coeditor of *Letters of Sherwood Anderson* (1953), *A College Book of Modern Verse* (1958), *A College Book of Modern Fiction* (1961), and *American Poetry* (1965). In 1981 he was a lecturer in English at the Kyoto American studies summer seminar. In 1983 he received the MidAmerica Award of the Society for the Study of Midwestern Literature. At present he is completing a critical biography of Sherwood Anderson for Oxford University Press.

MAUREEN RYAN is professor of English and dean of the honors college at the University of Southern Mississippi. She received a B.A. degree in American Studies at Pennsylvania State University in 1975, an M.A. in English from Temple University in 1978, and a Ph.D. from Temple in 1984. Her publications include *Innocence and Estrangement in the Fiction of Jean Stafford* (1987) and a fall, 1994, *Kenyon Review* article on Stafford's nonfiction. She has also published on the work of Willa Cather and many contemporary American women writers. She is working on a book on women and gender in the literature of the Vietnam War.

GAYLORD F